I0662242

I'm Still Standing Stories of Survival

Crissie Leonard

Published by 6 Figure Chics Publishing, 2024.

Table of Contents

I'm Still Standing
Stories of Survival
Contributors:

Tiffany McIntosh

Calvin McIntosh

Kacia Warren

Crissie Ann Leonard

Dr. Shannette Bone

TanTisha Mitchell

Shavonne Renee

Lavetta Dodd

Rashanda Mack-Kelly

Dr. C. Renee Coleman

Edited by: Meghan Roll

Published by 6 Figure Chics Publishing in Houston, TX

ISBN Number: 979-8-9911644-4-3 (sc)

Library of Congress Control Number: 2024924625

Foreword

In the pages of '*I'm Still Standing: Stories of Survival*,' you will find a tapestry of human endurance woven from the threads of real-life struggles and triumphs. This book is not just a collection of stories; it is a testament to the strength of the human spirit and the unwavering belief in the power of resilience.

As the author of this collection, I come before you not as a detached observer, but as someone who has walked through the shadows of adversity and emerged on the other side. My journey has been fraught with experiences that could easily have overwhelmed me - abuse, trauma, abandonment, poverty, and divorce. Each chapter of my life has presented its own set of challenges, each one seeming insurmountable at the time.

But amid the darkness, I found a guiding light that helped me navigate through the storm: my faith. Keeping God at the center of my life has been the cornerstone of my survival. It is through my relationship with God that I discovered a wellspring of strength and hope, an inner resilience that defied the odds and allowed me to stand tall in the face of adversity.

The stories within this book mirror my own experiences, reflecting the struggles and victories of others who have faced their own trials. They share a common thread: the refusal to be defined by the circumstances that sought to break them. These narratives are a celebration of perseverance, an exploration of the deep and unyielding courage that resides within us all.

As you read these stories, I hope you will find inspiration in the strength of those who have endured unimaginable hardships. Their journeys are a powerful reminder that even when life seems designed to bring us to our knees, there is always a path ahead - one illuminated by faith, resilience, and the unwavering will to keep moving forward.

In sharing my story and those of others, my deepest desire is that this book serves as a beacon of hope and a source of encouragement for anyone who finds themselves facing their own battles. We are all capable of rising above our challenges, and sometimes, the most profound strength comes from simply refusing to give up.

Thank you for joining me on this journey. May these stories inspire you to find your own inner strength and to remember that no matter what you face, you too can stand strong and keep moving forward.

With heartfelt gratitude and hope,

Tiffany McIntosh

Introduction

In 'I'm Still Standing: Stories of Survival', readers are invited into the raw, unfiltered experiences of men and women who confront life's most daunting adversities. This compelling collection of narratives explores the profound challenges that test their limits—whether battling against relentless natural elements, overcoming deeply personal struggles, or navigating through oppressive societal forces.

Each story reveals a different facet of human resilience as characters grapple with situations designed to break them. From harrowing survival in hostile environments to navigating the wreckage of personal loss and societal injustice, these accounts illuminate the indomitable spirit that keeps them moving forward.

The book shines a light on the transformative power of perseverance and the courage required to stand firm when everything seems to be conspiring against you. 'I'm Still Standing' offers a powerful testament to the strength found in vulnerability and the triumph of the human spirit. It's a celebration of endurance, hope, and the unwavering resolve to rise above even the most crushing circumstances.

Through these remarkable stories, readers are reminded that even when faced with overwhelming odds, the human capacity for survival and resilience is boundless. This collection not only inspires but also serves as a poignant reminder that we are all capable of standing strong against the storms life throws our way.

Chapter 1: From Darkness to Light: My Journey of Resilience
By: Lavetta Dodd

"Back in the days when I was young, I'm not a kid anymore, but some days I sit and wish I was a kid again...."

This song plays in my head more often than I'd like to admit, especially as an adult. It's a nostalgic reminder of a time when life seemed simpler, yet it's also a painful echo of a childhood marked by ridicule and body image struggles. Growing up, I was frequently mocked for my big lips and chubby frame. The taunts and jeers took root deep within me, fostering a sense of inadequacy and a belief that I was somehow flawed.

I was raised in a strict Pentecostal household where church was not just a part of life—it was life. The rules were clear: no earrings, no pants, no makeup. My life was one of strict adherence to religious doctrine, leaving little room for self-expression or exploration. By the time I graduated high school, I was eager to break free from the constraints that had bound me for so long. I wasn't wild, but I was ready to rebel against the rigid upbringing I had known.

The Allure of Independence: First Love and Heartbreak

My newfound freedom led me into the arms of my first boyfriend—a man older and, in hindsight, far more experienced in the ways of the world than I was. My brother despised him, warning me against the relationship, but his disapproval only fueled my determination. After all, this was my first taste of independence, my first chance to prove that I could handle the world on my own terms.

Our relationship lasted six months, and when it ended, I thought I was prepared for the world of adult relationships. The next man I dated shattered that illusion by breaking up with me for being "too nice."

The words cut deep, leaving me feeling once again unworthy. But I pressed on, learning about love and life through a series of relationships over the next few years.

When I met the father of my oldest son, I thought I had finally found stability. We had a beautiful son together, but the relationship crumbled under the weight of infidelity. My body image issues and trust issues, already fragile, were now magnified tenfold.

The Descent: Love, Control, and the Thug I Thought I Needed

Then along came Darren. He was everything I didn't know I wanted—dangerous, thrilling, and, as I would soon learn, destructive. Being with Darren was like riding a rollercoaster: exhilarating highs followed by stomach-churning lows. The first time he laid hands on me, I was shocked, dismayed, and utterly confused. How could someone who claimed to love me inflict such pain?

In hindsight, I see now that this was the beginning of his control over me. He explained away his actions, twisting my thoughts until I believed that somehow, it was my fault. The grounded, rational part of me knew better, but the broken, insecure part of me swallowed his excuses whole. I don't even remember what triggered that first violent outburst. All I recall is the searing pain and the chilling realization that my life had taken a dark turn.

But not everything was bad—how could it be? We were together for over a decade, after all. We moved in together, blending our families into one chaotic household with four kids. But with every step deeper into this life with him, the isolation grew, and so did his control. He would tell me that no one could love me like he did, and in the ways that mattered to me then, I believed him.

The next major blow-up occurred in front of my little sister and her friends. We retreated to a room to talk, but once the door closed, the discussion turned violent. He choked me, his hands squeezing the life out of me as he vowed to teach me a lesson for disrespecting him. In that moment, a part of me died. I begged him to end it—to kill me, to release me from this hell—but he didn't. Instead, he let me live, and I was left to pick up the shattered pieces of my spirit.

The Cycle of Abuse: Bruises and Broken Trust

My brother, always my protector, confronted me after that incident. He sat me down, looked me in the eye, and said, "Sis, I will gladly intervene, but if I do, you better not go back." His words hit me like a ton of bricks. How dare he question my resolve? How could he think I would stay after being choked? But deep down, I knew he was right.

Still, I stayed. And in an odd twist, the next few months were peaceful. We even moved to a bigger apartment to accommodate our growing family. But peace in my life was always temporary, a brief respite before the storm. Darren's infidelities continued, and with each new betrayal, my humiliation deepened. I didn't know which was worse: the bruises left by his fists, or the wounds inflicted by his cheating.

Our next fight was one for the record books—horrible and degrading. It started over money, as many of our fights did. He wanted help fixing his car, and when I told him I didn't have any extra cash until payday, he snapped. He pushed my head into the closet so hard that I fell inside. We fought, literally, in that small, enclosed space, with his brothers standing by, egging him on.

I bit him, clinging to his flesh like a lifeline, until one of his brothers finally pulled him off me.

After they left, I called my mom to pick up my sister and son. I couldn't bring myself to explain why, but she came. That night, despite the bruises and the pain, I went out with friends, trying to forget the horror of what had just happened. But Darren wouldn't leave me alone. He called incessantly, begging to talk things over. Against my better judgment, I let him come over. We talked, I cried, he explained, and I forgave. And so, the cycle continued, each turn of the wheel driving me deeper into despair.

The Breaking Point: A Child Lost, a Soul Shattered

When I found out I was pregnant again, I thought maybe, just maybe, things would change. For a while, they did. The physical abuse subsided, though the cheating did not. We moved to a house, hoping for a fresh start. But the peace was short-lived.

One morning, after another late-night return from Darren, we argued over his disrespectful behavior. I told him that a respectable man would come home to his pregnant girlfriend. He laughed at me, his derision palpable, and then he struck. He smashed my head into the bathroom door with such force that I saw stars. I was carrying his child, and yet, he didn't care. He laughed it off, saying he didn't hit me—he pushed me.

The worst was yet to come. A few months later, on Mother's Day, we were at his brother's house. I wasn't feeling well, but I tried to push through, hoping to enjoy the day. But Darren, always the master of control, found fault in something as trivial as where I was standing in the room. He berated me all the way home, accusing me of seeking attention, of being out of order.

That night, I went to bed confused and hurt, unable to understand why he was so angry.

The next day, at work, my water broke. It was too soon—far too soon. My coworkers called 911, and I called Darren, telling him to meet me at the hospital. When he arrived, the doctors told us that I needed to be on bed rest for the remainder of my pregnancy. But it was too late. My labor started, and at 22 weeks, our son, Jordan, was born. He didn't survive.

Darren's reaction was a mix of anger and blame. He left the hospital, leaving me alone in my grief. When I returned home, he stood over me with a belt, accusing me of killing our son. He beat me, saying he could never forgive me, that he hated me. My already fragile spirit shattered. I couldn't understand how someone who once claimed to love me could inflict such pain, especially after such a devastating loss.

That day, I made a vow to myself: I would no longer let him hit me without consequences. I called his mother, telling her that if he ever touched me again, I would send him back to her in pieces. I was done being his punching bag.

The Road to Recovery: Healing and Rebuilding

The next year was a blur of depression and despair. I would lie in bed all day, unable to summon the strength to face the world. Only an hour before Darren and DJ were due home would I force myself up to clean the house and start dinner, pretending that everything was fine.

It wasn't until my mother intervened that I realized I needed help. She encouraged me to join a grief support group, and for a while, it helped.

But Darren, the controlling force in my life, insisted that I stop. So, I did.

Then, a glimmer of hope—I became pregnant again. This time, things were different. I was back at work, and although Darren was still cheating, the physical abuse had stopped. We moved once more, this time to a bigger house with a yard for our growing family. Our baby girl was born in 1998, perfect in every way. For a time, we were content. But happiness? That was something I could only find in my children. Darren and I merely existed together, going through the motions of a life that had long since lost its joy.

By the Turn of the Millennium

I was done with our "shacking up," as the church folks called it. I wanted us to be married, believing that perhaps our living in sin was the root of our problems. Darren resisted, arguing that we didn't need a piece of paper to validate our relationship. But I stood my ground, and eventually, he agreed.

The Final Straws: Cutting Ties and Reclaiming My Life

The night before our wedding, Darren was out cheating. I knew it, but I married him anyway. Looking back, I wonder how much more I could have taken before I broke completely. After everything—years of abuse, betrayal, and humiliation—he was the one who left me. He walked away, leaving me to pick up the pieces of my shattered life.

But his leaving was the best thing that ever happened to me. It forced me to look inward, to rebuild myself from the ground up. I turned to books by Iyanla Vanzant, devouring her wisdom as I worked to heal my broken spirit.

Piece by piece, I put myself back together, stronger and wiser than before.

Embracing Strength and Finding Peace

Today, I live with a positive mindset. Yes, life still has its challenges, but I face them with the knowledge that I am strong, capable, and worthy. I have worked hard to rebuild my body image, embracing the truth that I am fearfully and wonderfully made. I know now that nothing God creates is flawed.

I speak affirmations over my life daily, setting a positive example for my children. I raised them in a healthy, loving environment, determined to show them what unconditional love looks like. My daughter, especially, needed to see how a woman should be treated—with respect, kindness, and love.

If there is one thing, I want others to take from my story, it is this: strength. The strength to endure, to rise above, and to reclaim your life, no matter how dark the path may seem. Every situation can change for the better, but it starts with you.

I'll leave you with one of my favorite verses from the Bible:

Jeremiah 29:11 (NIV): "For I know the plans I have for you," declares the Lord, "plans to prosper you and not to harm you, plans to give you hope and a future."

I know the Lord has a calling on my life, and my story will heal some and free others. Be blessed, and always stay grounded in God.

About the Author

Born in Kansas City, Missouri in May of 1970, to Eddie Dodd and Ruby Hill, her parents' youthfulness never left her lacking in any way. Growing up in a blended family taught her that love is universal and that you don't have to give birth to a child to love them with your whole heart. She learned, by example, what real unconditional love looks like.

Proud mother of three children, Dion Moss Jr., Lajai Ivy, and DeAnthony Ivy, and grandmother of two amazing granddaughters, Ty'lia Robinson, and Laylona Cisneros-Moss, her motivation for everything in life is them. She's also been blessed with children from love, Derek Ivy Jr., Derrisha Ivy, and Derrius Ivy, who allow her to continue laying a foundation with blended hearts and families.

Owner and CEO of Beautifully Crafted Salon Spa and Care, her life's mission is to bring the spa and daycare model to the forefront. At Beautifully Crafted, the goal is for everyone to feel good about themselves while remaining healthy. The salon specializes in natural hair, but also caters to wig and weave installations. Taking a holistic approach, Beautifully Crafted helps everyone access their inner vibrations to stay aligned, offering childcare for employees and clients, ensuring a supportive environment for all.

LaVetta's passion will always be to help the next woman see her strength. You never know how strong you are until strong is all you must be. Seeing your power even during your storms causes you to dig deep and overcome all obstacles.

As the Bible says in Isaiah 54:17 NIV: "No weapon forged against you will prevail, and you will refute every tongue that accuses you. This is the heritage of the servants of the Lord, and this is their vindication from me," declares the Lord.

Ultimately, while there may be challenges, no one can stop what God has for you. Lavetta would like to thank her family, clients, and all the strong women she has encountered, as you are her inspiration and drive; striving to give back by fostering a community of strength, beauty, and love.

Connect with me:

Facebook- Vetta Dodd-Ivy

Quote and Scripture

Our deepest fear is not that we are inadequate.

Our deepest fear is that we are powerful beyond measure.

It is our light, not our darkness

That most frightens us.

We ask ourselves

Who am I to be brilliant, gorgeous, talented, fabulous?

Actually, who are you not to be?

You are a child of God.

You're playing small

Does not serve the world.

There's nothing enlightened about shrinking

So that other people won't feel insecure around you. -**excerpt from Our Deepest Fear by Marianne Williamson**

Jeremiah 29 :11-"For I know the plans I have for you," declares the Lord, "plans to prosper you and not to harm you, plans to give you hope and a future."

Chapter 2: I Surv5ived
By: Dr. Shannette Bone

I am a woman who has been broken since I was a little girl. At the age of 15, I had my first son, and my second son a year and a half later. As a young woman, I did my best to survive. I sold drugs and was in abusive relationships with older men in my attempt to find love. At age 16 I was sexually assaulted and at 23 I was blessed to have my first daughter. By the age of 26, I gave birth to my last daughter.

Growing up in a drug-infested area, I sold drugs to survive. I was a young teen mother with limited options to provide for my children. While they never did anything illegal, they suffered because I did. The consequences of being arrested by the police and charged with the distribution of cocaine were that I spent 30 days in jail. Since I was charged without evidence, the case was dismissed by the judge. I was released after making the bail bond, which is when I had an encounter with God. I knew I had to break the generational curse and change the trajectory for my children. My children never got involved with the streets nor did they do drugs. They all went to school, played sports, graduated with honors, and by God's grace, all four of them went to college. As of today, three have graduated college, while my youngest daughter is a sophomore. I decided to move to the suburbs of my city and was approved to stay in Section Eight Housing where I lived on food stamps. During this time, I encountered men who were mentally, emotionally, and physically abusive.

While I was seven months pregnant with my eldest daughter, an ex-boyfriend who had recently been released from prison began to harass me.

He threatened that if he couldn't have me, no one could, and chased me with a gun, targeting me and my two young sons. In a desperate bid to protect my children, I threw them over a fence and fled, abandoning my truck. I fell on my stomach during the chaos. A family friend who was driving by and picked up me and my two sons and rushed us to the hospital. My siblings came to pick up my sons, to ensure no harm would come to them.

While I stayed in the hospital for observation, I heard a knock on the door. Naked, trying to change out of my regular clothes into my hospital gown, I said hold on, assuming it was the doctor. To my horror, it was the abusive man who had harassed me earlier. Panicked and frightened, he came in with a bouquet of flowers trying to apologize. I quickly pressed the alert button to summon security, while he ran out the hospital. Though they never caught him, when I was eventually released from the hospital I pressed charges against him; 13 different charges related to his threats against me and my children.

Despite working dead-end jobs and struggling to make ends meet, I continued to persevere. After nine years of living in Section Eight Housing, I was informed that I would need to start paying rent out of my own pocket. Faced with this new challenge, I decided to buy the house I was living in, though the owner's asking price was high.

Taking a leap of faith, I chose to purchase my first home and re-built it from the ground up.

I began remodeling my home in 2015 and completed the process in March 2016. Despite only working at my job for two weeks with a pay rate of $12.00 an hour, I managed to get approved for the house, a feat that surprised many. When questioned about my approval, I confidently replied that I knew someone "Who sits high and looks low."

After several years at that job, I was presented with a government job opportunity that paid $26.15 an hour. I saw it as a significant opportunity, though I soon discovered the challenges of working in corporate America, especially as a young, attractive, single mother.

As time went on, I faced more difficulties, including the loss of relatives to violence and natural causes. I met a man who I thought was the love of my life. We dated, and I co-signed for a truck for him. Although we often visited each other, I traveled more frequently because I was free on weekends and my children were older. We got engaged, but his inability to change his old habits led to our separation. Consequently, I ended up taking back the truck and was left with the payments.

As time passed, my former partner and I continued to stay in touch and see each other. In September 2020, he was involved in a severe accident and fell into a medically induced coma.

He spent nearly a month in the hospital, and I decided to take an unpaid leave of absence to support him and help him recover. I used my 401(k) to cover household expenses while I was away.

Once he recovered, he resumed seeing multiple women, leaving me devastated. About six months later, while attending a conference in Fort Lauderdale, Florida, I flew back to Nashville but found myself unable to walk when I deplaned. A kind man at the airport helped me, and I managed to drive home. Upon arriving home, I discovered that my daughter was back from college. She took me to the hospital.

After several tests and five days of uncertainty, the doctors diagnosed me with symptomatic lupus. Overcome with tears and unable to speak, I spent 15 days in the hospital. Despite my diagnosis, I continued to write and encourage others through my struggles. When I was finally discharged, I returned home with a walker and began therapy three times a week as therapists came to my house.

In August, the man I deeply loved came to my home and treated me harshly, questioning when I would start going to the gym and walking again. On August 2, 2021, he walked out on me, saying he would never call me again. Devastated, I cried and questioned God, who answered, "The man I have for you is tailor-made. He will love you for who you are—flaws, strengths, and everything in between. I had to show you what you don't want and who doesn't deserve you."

In the aftermath, I began writing and journaling, capturing every pain, fear, and betrayal.

I created a T-shirt featuring a Phoenix, symbolizing rising from the ashes, to represent my resilience and the strength of my family, including my four children. The number 5 on the shirt stood for grace and mercy—my sources of strength.

In December 2021, I earned my doctorate in humanities. Despite the ongoing pain of seeing my former partner marry someone else in February, I realized this was a necessary step. I had nearly settled to become his fifth wife, but I knew God had a different plan for me. Determined not to settle, I shifted my focus from my pain to my purpose, using it as fuel to change the trajectory of my life. I resolved that, despite everything I had been through, God would make my name great, and He would receive the glory from my story.

After I lost the ability to walk and bathe myself, I reached a point where I didn't want to be here anymore. But God told me, "Your story isn't just for you; it's for someone else. In life, you have three choices: your yard, the prison yard, and the graveyard. Choose wisely. While we all eventually face the grave, there's no need to rush toward it. I said no to premature death because you weren't fit to die just yet. Your story needs to be heard to help others. Remember, iron sharpens iron, and you can't be sharpened if you're surrounded by butter knife people."

Everything designed to break me contributed to making me exactly who I am today. From a young age, my desire has always been to make a difference and impact the world. Every stumble, block, and detour were God's way of showing me that the journey was bigger than myself. I was moving from generational curses to generational wealth.

I want to encourage you: don't stay where you're not valued. Go where you're celebrated, not just tolerated. Set healthy boundaries because one bad decision can either make or break you. I survived what might have killed someone else and lived to share my story of overcoming adversity. So, keep rising and soaring like that Phoenix. I traded beauty for ashes, and instead of breaking down, I broke through. Remember to live, laugh, and love, and be great even when faced with hate. If you want change, start by changing your mind to transform your life.

About the Author

Dr. Shannette Bone, a native of Huntsville, Alabama, has emerged as a beacon of resilience and empowerment within her community. Raised in an environment fraught with drug distribution, Dr. Bone was confronted with the challenge of raising her four young children as a single parent. Recognizing the need for a transformative change in their lives, she made the pivotal decision to relocate to the suburbs of Huntsville, disrupting their comfort zone and ushering in a new chapter.

Through unwavering determination and sacrifice, Dr. Bone successfully guided all four of her children through college, a remarkable achievement in itself. In 2021, she attained her Doctorate in Humanitarian Studies, furthering her commitment to making a difference in the lives of others.

Dr. Bone's dedication to her community extends beyond her nonprofit work. In her role as a leader with Faith In Action Alabama and her involvement with Chill Huntsville's "Stop the Violence" initiative, she actively contributes to creating a safer and more harmonious society. She received award nominee in 2021-2022 Women Breaking barriers. She also was a 2023-2024 NAACP recipient. A recipient from women's history month. A recipient for sister of the year award nominee for Atlanta, Georgia which that reward will be September 28, 2024. Congratulations to Dr. Shannette Bone for her 2024 DWAP Award nominations that will take place October19, 2024 in North Carolina. Her 2024 DWAP Awards nominations include:

- Entertainer of the Year
- Influencer of the Year
- Podcast of the Year
- Social Media Impact
- Woman of the Year
- Woman Owned Business

Keynote Speaker Dr. Shannette Bone Miami, Florida October 21, 2024-◇◇◇◇◇◇ ◇◇◇◇◇ ◇◇◇◇◇ ◇◇◇◇◇◇ ◇◇◇ ◇◇◇◇ 2024!

<u>Connect with me</u>:

Facebook: DrShannetteBone

Instagram: DrShannetteBone

TikTok: @drahannettebone5

YouTube: Dr. Shannette Bone

Quote and Scripture

When you want to succeed as bad as you want to breath, then you will be successful.-Eric Thomas

Jeremiah 29 :11-"For I know the plans I have for you," declares the Lord, "plans to prosper you and not to harm you, plans to give you hope and a future."

Chapter 3: Gone From My Life Yet Still in My Heart

By: Kacia Warren

From an early age, I was surrounded by death. My first loss was my grandfather who was lovingly nicknamed Grandpa Jeffers. His affectionate smile beamed for me daily, especially since he lived with my family. Grandpa wore overalls every day and had a distinct smell, one you recognized when you entered a room. I sat on his lap and sang to him and was rewarded with his smile. He was 80 and certainly influenced my understanding of love.

I was too young to understand death when he passed. I knew it was upsetting, and he was gone though. His passing was very traumatic for me, but I found comfort in knowing he was in Heaven. To process through the emotions of his loss and too young to understand the powerful grip grief has, I talked to him daily. I told myself that Grandpa Jeffers would watch over me from heaven.

A domino effect took hold of my life after Grandpa Jeffers died. I watched and cared for those that made a lasting impression on my life. I spent many hours, days, and weeks taking care of my loved ones nearing the end of their lives. With each person, I grew to understand that death is part of the cycle of life. Accidents happen, people get sick, and doctors cannot save everyone. It is brutally painful to watch your loved ones losing their battles with sickness. You reciprocate the love and care they gave you by showing and giving comfort, compassion and respect to them. In the end you will do whatever is necessary to see them happy, loved, and comfortable.

While I was young and as I've grown older, I've felt peace in knowing that they went to a better place after departing Earth.

They were no longer in pain or struggled through their sickness. Instead, they went to Heaven to be with our God. This brings comfort to me when saying my final goodbyes to them. I somehow know that people are there waiting to usher them into Heaven and that my family members are safe in the loving arms of Jesus.

To say that this knowledge helped during the passing of my sister and mother would be a lie. Everything I experienced before could never prepare me for their deaths. Each was traumatic and left gaping wounds that have yet to heal. It felt like my heart was ripped from my chest and shredded into pieces, then thrown back inside me without any glue to put it back together!

To understand the level of trauma, you first need to know the circumstances surrounding their deaths. Both died in different ways and surrounded by other people, but the effect on me was excruciating.

My sister's name was Gidget. She was vibrant, full of life and everyone loved her. A tomboy that could hang with the boys and be your defender in a fight. She was always willing to defend those around her and seek justice for those who were wronged. Gidget's personality naturally drew people to her including my children, especially my son Aaron.

They had a special bond and were close to each other. This closeness made the day of her death even more unbearable. That Monday in August started as a beautiful day. The sun was shining, and the air held a vibrancy of life in it. Even the workday went well! But everything changed when the phone rang after work.

I was taking my daughter to feed horses in Pickaway County. We were enjoying the ride when the phone rang. It was from Aaron, my son. I answered only to hear him screaming that Aunt Gidget was blue. At first, I didn't realize what was happening because Aaron kept screaming on the phone. I tried to focus my mind to understand the situation. He was yelling that she was blue, and that he did not know how to perform CPR. Trying to focus on driving, while attempting to process what Aaron was saying; the tone of his voice told me it was an emergency. I told him to hang up and call 911 and I was on my way to him.

I told my daughter there was an emergency and we had to go back home. We would go feed the horses another day. Someone needed to go check on Gidget and Aaron. I frantically called home trying to reach my husband only to keep getting voicemail. Now I was frantic, irritated, and upset. Where was everyone when you needed them?

My mind was recalling people and their schedules like a phone rolodex. My best friend Kelly came to mind. I prayed she would answer as I dialed her number. After a few rings, Kelly answered.

My voice shook as I retold the conversation with Aaron to her and asked her to go to the house and check on them. I stressed this was an emergency and I really needed some help since I was not close to home. She agreed to go check on them and promised to call when she arrived.

My mind raced with thoughts and scenarios of what was happening. My heart was beating out of my chest as I felt a sense of dread and fear. I glanced at my daughter and knew I had to focus on driving safely. It was difficult to reign in my thoughts. They kept straying to the possibilities of what could have happened, and my anxiety increased with every mile I drove.

Normally the drive back home takes 45 minutes, but I made it in 20 minutes! I was making the turn onto the street when Kelly called me. She arrived and said it was a chaotic scene and getting to the house was difficult. Kelly advised me to park down the street and get there on foot. She had found Aaron, and he was in a frantic state. My mama bear instincts kicked in and nothing or no one would stop me from getting to my son!

I parked the car and ran towards the house. It looked like a three-ring circus when I turned the corner. Police and Fire trucks blocked the road. A large crowd formed near the house. I noticed the neighbors were there trying to see what was happening. I heard dogs barking, and the noise level was overwhelming! Even though Kelly prepared me for the chaotic scene, it was still unsettling!

I valiantly tried to hold myself together as I worked through the crowd. My only focus was to find Aaron! Instead of finding him first, I was met by my oldest son Austin, who was also in a panicked state. He was talking so fast that I had difficulty understanding him. I was desperate to find Aaron but torn with staying to soothe Austin. It felt like time froze as I struggled to choose between my two sons. In the end, I did my best to comfort Austin as I took him with me to find Aaron. I was willing to forcefully move people out of the way if necessary. We burst through the crowd at a frantic pace. I am sure it was a sight to behold!

I neared the house steps only to be stopped by a police officer. He asked me to leave, and I told him no. He stared at me for a minute, and I told him that I was not leaving until I spoke to my son. I moved past him and burst through the door. I stood in shock in the doorway as I processed the scene around me. What happened here?

I desperately scanned the room searching for Aaron. He was in the bedroom talking to a police officer. The medics stood nearby. I looked from the medics to the floor where a body was covered by a sheet. Sadness and shock descended on me, and I knew without any doubt that Gidget was under that sheet!

I moved closer to Aaron without imposing on his reporting to the police officers. He raised his eyes to me, and I saw the terror in them.

I felt helpless and knew this was a wound Aaron would carry for the rest of his life and no salve would heal it.

My emotions swirled like a storm brewing in the sea. How do I help my children? What do I tell my family? Where was my mother? That last thought came, and I realized that my mom was not home. A part of me was thankful that she did not experience this ordeal. Another part of me dreaded telling her the news of Gidget's death.

Thoughts of my family members came to mind, and I wondered how each of us would handle today's events. Gidget's death would be a shocking and devastating blow to our family. We knew she struggled with drugs, but not to the extent of an overdose. I called my husband and explained the situation. I asked him to pick mom up from her work; to tell her there was an emergency and bring her home.

I closed the blinds in preparation for the circus that was about to happen. Tears streamed down my face; I wiped them away and took deep breaths. My role would now be the ringmaster and I needed to regain control of myself to deal with my family. The next hours were filled with meetings with detectives, hazmat units, nosy neighbors, and television crews descending on our house. We were the breaking news, and our house was a crime scene for four days.

Everyone had their own interpretation of what happened or at least what they told themselves happened.

However, they did not understand the gravity of the events or face the truth of her overdose. My mother and children were devastated and in a state of mourning, while I was trying to survive and be the rock for everyone in my family.

Everyone eventually came to terms with Gidget's death. We mourned and went back to our daily life routines. But we were all scarred and changed from that night. Some days were better than others. I focused on raising my children as I dealt with the loss of my sister. The children resumed their lives. Mom went from living a vibrant life to being depressed and overweight. The aftermath of that night took a heavy toll on my family.

Other family members and friends would pass away in the next eight years. The weight of the never-fully addressed trauma from Gidget continued to grow heavier with each passing. I learned to heavily mask my pain through those years.

My family saw me as the rock. The one who was strong enough to lean on. In reality, I felt like a grain of sand, constantly being washed out to sea, and then returned to endure more. Where could I find a rock to lean on? Realizing that my family and friends could not be my rock, I turned to God. I deepened my relationship with Him, and my faith increased. A sense of peace finally settled within me. But that would be short-lived because the next domino of death was ready to fall during one of the happiest times of my life.

Wedding plans dominated my days and nights. I was eager to marry again with the man who brought sunshine to my darkest days over these past eight years. We would walk down the aisle and pledge our lives to each other! Then we would have an extended honeymoon in Greece. I was excited about all this and even more that my mom was able to attend my wedding despite her back injury.

Five days before the wedding, mom was having a simple outpatient lower laminectomy surgery for a pinched nerve in her back. We were the first people to arrive at the hospital. The paperwork was completed, and mom was taken to her "waiting" room. I was in the surgical waiting room with my girlfriend, who was a social worker at the hospital and sat with me before her shift that day. Having my best friend there to support me gave me comfort. It turned out that I would need her there for more than support that day.

To pass the time, I went through my wedding planner. Phone calls were made to vendors to confirm details and drop-off times. After I finished the multiple calls, I realized that no nurse came to update us on mom's surgery. We were now at the two-hour mark for a forty-five-minute surgery. That was a big red flag for me! I put my planner away and went to the nurses' station for an update. They did not have one, so I asked my friend to check the chart for any issues. Before my friend came back, they informed me that mom was heading to the recovery area.

They moved me to a different area to wait for the doctor. Hours passed and she had not woken from the anesthesia. Neither the doctor nor my friend came to give me any updates. Fear and anxiety set in as the waiting continued!

In an effort to curb my emotions, I reminded myself that it was Good Friday and Easter weekend - A time for miracles and I needed one right now! I continued to pray and remained hopeful for good news. I kept telling myself that we have plans for the future, so a quick recovery was needed. But deep down I had a feeling of dread which increased as the time continued to go by without an update.

I sought out a nurse again and asked to see my mother. Her reply was that mom was still resting and had yet to awaken from the anesthesia. I stood staring at her with an aghast expression on my face! What do you mean she is still sleeping? It has been eight hours since the surgery! The hair on my neck stood up and I knew something was terribly wrong. How can we be the first to arrive and the last to leave?

Finally, my name was announced. I headed to the cubicle where the doctor was waiting. I was ready with my questions. His next words were like freezing water being dumped on me -chilled me to the bone! He informed me that unfortunately he nicked her spine (fluid) while in surgery. They had to repair it with sure glue. My first thought was you must be kidding me! Then my barrage of questions began. Is that a normal procedure?

What happens next? How long is the recovery time? Is that even safe?

He answered that the recovery time would be longer than expected. It was a holiday weekend so they would keep her overnight to monitor her. I kept pressing him for answers to the other questions, but he was elusive with his answers. I was aggravated and went on high alert. Something was not right!

My girlfriend read the chart during her rounds and told me to ask more questions. Now, my anxiety was escalating, as was my concern level. I was led back to the surgical waiting room. The lady sitting across from me said she had been here all day too with her father. He had the same procedure and was still in recovery. Finally, someone I could chat with about the surgery and our parents. I told her I was from this local area, and she replied she was from Cincinnati.

Our parents were finally settled into their hospital rooms. We met again and went to dinner together. Neither of us understood how important our meeting was that night or how much we would need each other!

Both of our parents were uncomfortable and had rough nights. We met again the next morning in the hall as we were both searching for assistance. Our parents had the same doctor and surgery, and neither were doing well. My mom had a fever and became delirious. She was speaking things that did not make sense, struggling to stay awake, and was on extraordinarily little medication.

Mom constantly complained of being uncomfortable and in pain. Out to the hallway I went again; this time in search of medication for her. Our overnight stay turned into several days. She was finally discharged on Monday. The nurses taught me her wound care and directions for her medicine. Mom left the hospital a different person than when we arrived!

On the way home, Mom demanded we stop to purchase lottery tickets. We giggled and imagined ourselves becoming millionaires! When we arrived home, I got her settled in. She commented that her back pain and headache were getting worse. It was getting ready to storm, so we attributed it to the change in barometric pressure.

I showered, changed clothes, and went back to check on her. It was time to change her bandage. I did not understand feeling an overwhelming need to keep that bandage, but I did and placed it in a zip lock baggy. This decision would change everything!

Mom became increasingly irritable as the night progressed. She started sweating profusely and her heart rate kept rising. I panicked, thinking she was having a heart attack and called 911 requesting assistance and an e-squad. As I paced the floor waiting for them to arrive, I looked out the window. It was storming with downpouring rain. I was anxious trying to figure out how they were going to load my mom in the ambulance.

They arrived and despite the rain loaded mom into the ambulance with ease.

I did not want to go back to the hospital where the surgery was, so I requested to go to a different hospital. They granted my request. Upon arrival, we were immediately sent to the ER department. I had her previous medical history, current surgery details, and post-surgery instructions with me. I also brought the bandage in a baggy!

We were put in a private room away from everyone. They asked about her medications, ordinary questions about her, her pain threshold, duration of intense pain, and requested the bandage baggy. I informed them that she just spiked a fever and has had a horrible headache since we left the hospital. She was also delirious, incoherent when she spoke, and hallucinating in her pain.

I was terrified and could sense the urgency of the situation. Alone and trying to figure out this situation, hours went by before I realized that in my panicked state that I did not call anyone. I decided to wait until I had more answers before I alarmed anyone else. I stayed by my mom's side until they took her for testing.

They continued to take her for new tests. New doctors came to ask questions and then left. At this point, I am extremely alarmed with the situation. Not having answers was irritating me and raising my anxiety levels. They called the doctor that performed the surgery in their question to find answers. They continue to review her charts.

I sat with a blank stare on my face. My mind finally processed the gravity of the situation. I look at her lying restlessly in the bed with all the monitors and EKG lines hooked to her. Asking only pertinent questions so I did not disturb her. She was in a critical state, and I could not lose my mother!

Days later she was stabilized and moved to an isolation room on the fifth floor. My nerves were nonexistent at this point. This had been a harrowing ordeal, and it was not over yet! This new day started with doctor's rounds and more questions. I kept asking for a prognosis report. They informed me that they wanted to get mom stable so they could do a debrief session on her surgery. She had a bacterial infection which they believed was spinal meningitis, but they could not be sure until they were able to look into her spine for confirmation.

All the restless nights were finally catching up to me. I called my aunt to see if she would come sit with mom so I could go home to shower and gather myself. Then I helped get mom prepped for her surgery, but my body revolted, and I ran to the bathroom. I could hear them paging me, but I was not able to leave the bathroom right then. Someone came to the bathroom, and I asked them to please go out there and tell them I needed a few more minutes. I was sick to my stomach. In hindsight, I believe my body was preparing itself for what was to come.

My aunt came to the bathroom to check on me. I was a mess!

The stress had taken its toll on my body and mind. The weight of carrying this load was tremendous and I did not have any support. I finally got myself together and left the bathroom. They took mom away for surgery. My aunt and I began the waiting game. The nurses were fantastic, attentive, kind, caring, thoughtful, and considerate.

One nurse read the chart and handed me a post it note. It says keep this for your peace of mind. I look into her eyes and nod in understanding. She was bringing me peace and closure in this chaos. I googled what she gave me without telling anyone anything. The search helped me ask more pointed questions, while realizing the end result would be death.

The infectious disease doctor came, and we had a long, meaningful discussion about what would happen. There were no drugs available to treat this infectious disease. He explained that her organs would shut down one at a time. The shutdown speed depended on her ability to fight. I smiled because my mom is a Leo, and we are born fighters! I knew she would fight with all she had!

27

I knew we were in for a battle. I prayed up and put on the full armor of God. I finally made the phone calls to let everyone know her situation. As they all arrived to celebrate my mom, she slipped into a coma. I know she could hear the people in the room, as we recalled the good memories with laughter. I was thankful that she could not see all the tears being shed as everyone understood that she would not win this battle.

Mom slowly faded away. The doctors decided to send her to Hospice care on Monday. My heart shattered as I fully recognized that I was now saying goodbye to my mom. Tears escaped my eyes as I closed them, knowing that she would not be there to see me get married. I was not ready for her to leave me, so I climbed into her bed. As I cuddled her, I told her that I will be alright. She does not have to worry about me and stay here in pain. I had to take a few deep breaths before I could speak the next words to her. With a voice filled with agony, I told her that she could go home and be with her mom, brothers, sister, and everyone she loved. I told her that Gidget would be there waiting for her. With tears, hot as the sun, rolling from my cheeks onto her, I told her I loved her and will miss her dearly!

I hugged her one last time and climbed off the bed. I composed myself before asking for the priest to come in to bless her journey home. It is too painful to watch her hurting and dwindling away into nothingness. I prayed she would die peacefully in her sleep. I begged her to let go and be free. And yet, she continued to hold on.

It was Sunday afternoon and I wanted to go home to shower. My mom's friend was coming to sit with her while I was gone. I only lived six houses away, so I was close enough to return quickly if her situation changed. The nurse came in and after checking on mom she pleaded with me to go home and rest because I was emotionally, mentally, and physically exhausted. They gave me an Ativan. I could hear everything but struggled to keep my eyes open.

I knew I needed to rest, so I called my husband to pick me up. The nurse's words as she left the room were a foreshadowing that I missed. She told me that my mother would not die with me in the room. I nodded and walked out after her to wait for my husband in the pickup area.

I went home, showered, and fell asleep. I was not sure how long I was asleep before the phone rang. I dreaded answering it. My hands shook as I raised the phone to my ear. My heart shattered when the nurse told me my mom just passed away. I jumped out of bed like it was on fire! As I rushed to leave, I scolded myself with why I could not hold on longer with mom. Why did she die without me there? I was not sure I would ever forgive myself for not being there with her as she departed this world!

I drove back to the hospital, burst through the doors, and rushed to the elevators. I raced into my mom's room to find only the nurse sitting with her. I frantically searched for mom's friend Mary. I did not find her anywhere. My heart sank with the weight of knowing mom died alone! I felt like I let her down and now I was drowning in sorrow. I cried out to the Lord for help and told Him I needed him now. Slowly walking towards the bed, I could only stare at my mom. I sat in the chair beside her bed and held her hand. The finality of her situation dawned on me, and I thanked God for taking mom home. I praised His name and through my tears I knew she was safe. I thanked Him again.

A sense of relief flooded over me because I knew she was celebrating on Heaven's streets of gold. A slow smile crept on my lips as I envisioned her singing His praises and greeting her family and friends.

I am unsure how much time has passed before the nurse came back into the room. A sense of peace enveloped me when I heard the nurse say that my mom knew how much I loved her. She would be proud of me and the strangers who came to the rescue in an effort to save her. I thanked the nurse and crawled back in bed with my mom. I needed time to hug her and gather my thoughts. Sometime later, I left the bed to sit in the chair and await the doctors.

They came and started asking critical questions about mom. They asked for permission to use her body for research. They expressed their desire to perform a study on her care to make improvements. No autopsy would be performed, and she would be cremated after the study. A piece of her brain would go to research labs to create new antibiotics. Mom was drug resistant which was extremely rare. I was honored that mom could contribute to improving medical care. Then out of nowhere I realized that I must cancel my wedding and plan her funeral instead!

It was determined that my mom contracted an Acinetobacter infection. According to a journal publication from 2021, a comprehensive review of data identified 198 patients with Acinetobacter baumanni. The prevalence of Acinetobacter baumanni is 3.37% and the overall mortality rate is 40.81%.

Another article stated that Acinetobacter baumanni is different because it is particularly tough. It is one of the most resistant pathogens encountered. My Mother was now a statistic!

You never know how strong you are or your will to survive until you experience traumatic events. I buried every loved one in my family. I had the sweet blessing of time to spend with each of them before they passed away. You come to understand that in life there is the good and bad, the beautiful and ugly, and eventually the demise of death. You are forced to confront how you see people, connect with them, and how you build relationships (hopefully long-lasting ones) with them.

I live in the moments, celebrating life and finding joy every day! Knowing that tomorrow is never promised and today is the day to connect with others and find joy. Understanding that death brings anger, what-if questions, and unfinished business. You reflect on every conversation, argument, and fight. Every moment of your life is analyzed hoping to numb the pain. The weight of your life's decisions and the overthinking of what could have been is a high price to pay! I certainly analyze things differently after these experiences. I survived all of these, and I am STILL STANDING! Proverbs 31:25 states, "She is clothed in strength and dignity and laughs without fear of her future." I evolved into a Proverbs 31 woman!

Throughout the years, I learned to become more compassionate and understanding and less judgmental.

To listen to and understand conversations instead of debating them. To give clarity to each question asked of me. Before ending a visit, say I LOVE YOU and give a hug to the people/person you are with. Let them know you value them and appreciate them in your life. It is important for people to understand where they stand with you while they are alive. It is too late to tell them when they die!

Tragic unexpected deaths leave you bewildered and without closure. My neighbor passed of an aneurysm while jumping on a trampoline with her daughter. She was full of life one moment and gone the next. That sudden death leaves your world in turmoil. It changes in an instant and you are unable to find closure. Instead, you must find a way to continue without them! I have friends that lost their children. They were left heartbroken and inconsolable!

We must find a way to push through and move on with our lives. While I agree that time does help heal wounds, the hole in your heart never goes away. Talking about your loved ones does eventually bring peace, but the level to which you miss them never decreases. Clawing through grief and getting out of bed each day is challenging. Grief can hit you like a tidal wave one day and affect you less on a different day. Each of us processes grief, pain, and trauma differently. What connects us is knowing that our loved ones would want us to move forward and live our lives. It is important to remember that you matter, and you can live your life in honor of them.

In times when we feel alone, let us reflect on Psalm 112:7, "She confidently trusts the Lord to care for her."

I found my calling when I put my pain into my purpose, which is telling my story of losing everyone in my family and how it affected my life. It started with my sister and her unexpected overdose and ended with losing my mom in 17 days from a hospital acquired infection. I also speak to losing my alcoholic father who drank himself to death. People need to understand the deep levels of trauma associated with the pain of losing people in our lives. Each loss and its circumstances changed me and the trajectory of my life.

I want people to be inspired by my journey. To understand that many times the only decision you have is to pick up the pieces and keep moving forward. To offer forgiveness to free yourself, not for the benefit of the other person. Seeing how a change in your mindset and attitude can transform your life! God granted me serenity and pulled me through the darkest times of my life. He showed me how to move forward in peace and with grace. I discovered that laughter could change a moment in your life. I am fully aware that sometimes a smile masks the pain buried deep inside. Most importantly, I learned to value those meant to be in my life and let those go that do not add value. As an empath, I feel and connect deeply with others. It requires a lot of energy and focus to serve those needing connection.

Often it drains me, and I need a healthy outlet and safe relationships to recharge. My strength comes from prayer, and knowing the Lord will never fail me!

Imagining that happiness can be found after painful experiences is hard to comprehend. But happiness is an inside job and dependent on you. It requires you to work on your personal growth daily. Tap into your strength, compassion, and intuition. Know who you are living for now. Do this with gratitude and it will turn everything you have into enough!

I am truly blessed and do things that set my soul on fire for God. When you are in doubt remember that Matthew 19:26 tells us that all things are possible with God!

I am thankful for my family and for being with them at the end of their lives. I had a gravestone cross done on my back. It reminds me that they are with me even when life is difficult! Life is full of challenges and if it does not challenge you, it will not change you! Life is a choice, so choose to live it in happiness and without regret. Live in each moment, especially with others. You will need those memories one day! Let God guide people into and out of your lives . That is His way of taking care of us!

Most importantly, you are strong enough to handle what life throws at you! Strength is born out of hardship. Endurance is born from difficulty. You were born with a purpose and for greatness. Always believe you can survive no matter the circumstances, no matter how big they are!

Remember that David slew Goliath in the Bible with a single shot from a slingshot. HE DID IT AND SO CAN YOU!

About the Author

Kacia Warren is an Accountability and Empowerment Strategist, Publicist, and Partner in Humble Heartbeat Publishing, L.P. She understands that the key to accomplishing your goals and finishing your tasks is accountability. Having someone to hold you accountable and help you focus on the tasks needed to accomplish the goal is the KEY to success!

She specializes in developing leadership skills, habit stacking, time blocking for task completion, creating accountability plans and schedules, marketing, and building relationships (business and personal) through personal development and Enneagram management.

Kacia is an avid reader and podcast listener. She loves books, podcasts, and volunteering in her community. Kacia has been featured on the cover of Triumphant Magazine, was a LitCon Author and Speaker (in both Alabama and Atlanta) and is a faithful servant for My Sisters Keeper Retreat in Orlando, Floria. Her speaking credits include Keynote Speaker for the Declare and Decree at Sea cruise onboard Carnival Cruise Lines and the Spotlight Speaker for HerSpark Summit. Kacia has also been named one of the Top Women in Business and Ministry for 2024.

As a master of networking, Kacia works with authors to develop branding, marketing strategies, and promoting their books and services. Partaking in an author's journey, she has gained wisdom and understanding for the challenges authors face from conception, to writing the book, to

publishing and promoting. She strives to instill in authors the importance of building relationships, networking, and employing associated marketing strategies. Kacia helps them draft a creative content plan to increase opportunities to grow their visibility and find their loyal fans!

Kacia identified the need for authors, especially first-time ones, who were seeking assistance with writing and publishing their books. She partnered with a writing coach to offer guidance with composition and accountability to authors in the early stages of their book writing journey. Their work together helped authors to achieve their dreams! As a co-owner in Humble Heartbeat Publishing, L.P., Kacia assists authors with publishing their books and developing marketing strategies by utilizing her publicist expertise.

Investing in yourself is a powerful commitment! Her message is "Yes you can, I BELIEVE in you!" Everyone wants to grow and become the best version of themselves, but often do not know where to start. Kacia believes it starts with a choice, then creating and following action steps to consistently work towards your vision and goals. Being dedicated to this path helps lead you to the results you want to see!

Often times our journey is derailed by the pain we experience in life. Kacia experienced this during a battle with grief and mourning. She was overwhelmed by the emotional turmoil and searched for a way to right herself back onto her path. Leaning into her faith, she learned to turn her pain into purpose with God's divine plan for her life.

Kacia's advice is focus on you, by building a healthy and positive mindset, seek emotional intelligence training, and learn to forgive others with grace to set yourself free. Lean into your faith and find the peace you are seeking!

And remember that the biggest believer you need is yourself!

Connect with me:

Facebook: Kacia Warren

Instagram:@coachkacia

Lemon8: @kaciawarren

Email:coachkacia@gmail.com

Quote and Scripture

All That I Am or Hope to Be, I Owe to My Angel Mother.-Abraham Lincoln

Psalm 46:5-"God is within her, she will not fall; God will help her at break of day."

Chapter 4: The Battle Within
By: Rashanda Mack-Kelly

It is truly by God's grace that I can occupy this space. You see, what the devil meant to harm me, God has used for my good. Every battle that I have faced in life has provoked me to PREVAIL! As I write this insert, I am currently battling Stage Two breast cancer. This is my second diagnosis of breast cancer. My first diagnosis was back in 2012; Stage Three breast cancer at the age of 33. I can remember the day of my diagnosis like it was yesterday. I took one of my closest friends with me to the doctor's appointment. I had the biopsy more than a week prior and it seemed to take forever awaiting the results. Before we arrived at the doctor's office, I was full of anxiety and needed something to calm my nerves. My friend and I stopped at the gas station because I wanted to get a pack of cigarettes. Yes, I used to smoke. I enjoyed the Newport Menthol Blue pack, 100's to be exact.

When I got to the doctor's office, there was a brief delay in getting to meet with my doctor. Once my name was called, we went in the back. I was overwhelmed with fear as we walked into the room. My friend and I sat quietly awaiting my doctor's arrival. After a few minutes of waiting, an unfamiliar doctor walked in the room. He introduced himself as Dr. Kelly. He explained to me that my doctor was stuck at the hospital in surgery and that he would be the one to give me the results of my biopsy. Honestly, I felt a sense of relief that this strange doctor was the one providing my results. In my mind, if the results would be unfavorable, surely my physician would be the one to advise me, not some strange doctor who I had never met and who did not know anything about my medical history.

Dr. Kelly picked up my medical records and scanned them briefly while saying uh-huh, ok. Then, he removed his glasses and placed them on the corner. "Ok, this is what we have here." He gained my undivided attention at that moment. Following those words, I heard" Stage three in situ carcinoma." He dropped my medical records on the counter and stared deep into my eyes. I felt like I had fallen into a trance. It even sounded like everything got extremely quiet for a moment. Then suddenly, there was a knock on the room door. It was Dr. Redcross, my actual physician. He could tell by the look on my face that I had already received my results. Both my friend and I looked clueless as to what would happen next. Dr. Redcross' proposed treatment plan was extremely aggressive. The plan included chemotherapy, radiation and surgery, but it was too much information to process all at once. I was still in complete shock by my results. With a history in the medical field, I knew that my diagnosis was some type of cancer, but I was in denial. I was too young to die. My children needed me. My elderly grandfather depended on me to be his caregiver. Now suddenly, I found myself on death row; literally waiting to die. After Dr. Redcross discussed the plan of action for treatment with us, my friend and I left. I honestly don't remember the ride back home. Once home, I sat quietly in fear. I was terrified that if I slept, I would die.

I could not eat for days, agonizing over dying and leaving my kids with no one reliable to care for them.

I believe that most people would be depressed, stressed, and/or ready to give up if they were in my situation. The difference is that I was hand-picked for a time such as this to help heal, deliver, and set free every captive bound by cancer.

People often only see the healed version of a cancer patient- the one who's made it through chemotherapy, radiation, surgery and recovery. But they don't see the struggle it took to get there. Unless you are a caregiver, you don't get to see the ugly and difficult parts of fighting cancer or any disease for that matter. I did, indeed, battle depression during my first encounter with cancer. I did not have the support system that I needed. My mother and maternal grandmother were deceased. I truly felt alone and somewhat defeated.

I cried daily asking God, "Why me?" I had starved myself for so long, that once I finally was able to eat, I would vomit everything back up that I had eaten. I could not even keep water down. I had lost so much weight, I looked and felt sick. People that knew me would stare at me, recognizing the weight loss. I was so depressed, and it showed.

I had friends that knew about my sickness, but they could not relate. I needed a support system. However, no one around me could offer what I needed at the time.

Hell, I didn't even know what I needed at the time. I just wanted something or someone to help me navigate what I would later find was my "new norm."

People would call me to check up on me, but they rarely had the right [comforting] words to say. Truthfully, I didn't want to do much talking during this time anyway. I needed something to soothe this pain from within. I needed to find ways of coping to overcome this pit that I had found myself in.

Reminiscing back to my childhood, I thought about times that my beloved grandma used to take me to church with her. As a kid, I was known as an intercessor in the church. The elders would often request for me to pray at the beginning of a service. Ironically, I can remember one elder in the church asking me for a "copy" of my prayer one Sunday. The audacity that he would think that I wrote these prayers. These prayers came straight from my heart to God's ears. I learned the words of an effective prayer from my grandma, Helen. She was a powerful woman of God with a sharp prophetic gift. Strangely, even she was afraid of her gift. She was fearful of how people would view her after she spoke what God told her to say. Oh, if I could be half the woman that my grandmother was.

I knew that I needed these prayers to get through this battle and if God could not do it, no one could. I began to search for scriptures on healing to declare over my life. Some of those scriptures included: Jeremiah 17:14 (NIV), "Heal me, Lord, and I will be healed; save me and I will be

saved, for you are the one I praise." Another one of the healing scriptures is Isaiah 53:5 (NIV), "By His wounds we are healed." Glory to God, Jesus had already died for our deliverance from sickness, and I believed it. As God began His inner works within, it was an uncomfortable process. He guided me through internal healing, but I could also see myself healing externally.

It's not easy to self-evaluate without boundaries. Most people find it easier to point the finger at others to make themselves feel better. During my healing process, I felt like God was doing something much greater in my life. I connected with a cancer support group to seek different ways to cope with my situation. I even began sharing my story with others as a testimony of what great works God had done in my life. During this time, my story was delivered in a way that seemed like a "woe is me" story instead of one of triumph.

It was a few years before I had a fresh revelation that this victory was much bigger than me. I realized that God was using me as a vessel to help others overcome and live victorious lives. He took me to the scripture: Luke 10:19 (NIV), "I have given you authority to trample on snakes and scorpions and to overcome all the power of the enemy; nothing will harm you." This meant I had the God-given authority to command cancer to wither in the name of Jesus, and it must submit to His name. It is crucial to first recognize and embrace the authority we have been given.

We must believe that we can take that authority and dispatch it to do the good things that God has given us the power to do. It is our birthright. So, with that understanding, diagnosed about seven months ago for the second time, I knew that this was BIGGER THAN ME. I honestly knew this before this diagnosis, but God was going to use me to get His glory this time around again! I could not walk in fear. I needed to be absolutely certain that He is who He says He is.

I have a very supportive husband who wants to see me thrive in every area of my life. He understands that I am a byproduct of him, and he is a byproduct of me. We understand the institution of family and the benefits of a healthy marriage. I know what I have endured was for my good, even if some days it did not appear that way. I made a conscious decision that I would turn my pain into purpose. I partnered with the American Cancer Society to spread awareness to families of the many resources that the American Cancer Society provides. I was able to pour into survivors like me and share the triumph of defeating this deadly disease. During this season, I learned that I had a genetic mutation. This meant that I was born with a cancerous gene that placed me at greater risk for cancer, specifically breast cancer. I never knew anything about the possibility of a genetic mutation until then. I was offered the testing during my first diagnosis, but my insurance declined to pay for it. It is imperative that we know our health status.

Often, we see our loved ones die from diseases, such as cancer, not realizing that it could run in our families.

Cancer ran into the wrong girl at the right time. I watched my maternal grandmother die from pancreatic cancer, while my mother was victorious over skin cancer.

Transparent Moment:

2 Corinthians 1:4-7 In this scripture, Paul explains that God comforts us in all our troubles. I believe that this divine comfort is not just for our relief, but it also serves a much greater purpose. It endows and equips us to comfort one another in difficult times. I am a firm believer that when we are transparent about our struggles and how we continuously receive God's comfort, we can effectively comfort and encourage others who experience similar battles.

Transparency in my Trauma:

If I am being honest, dealing with breast cancer has been a journey filled with deep insecurity and trauma. As I began motivational speaking 12 years ago to inspire, empower, and encourage other women, I uncovered layers of hidden pain that I had not fully acknowledged or processed. Through this period, God removed the scales from my eyes, revealing and healing the trauma from the inside out. This newfound freedom (mental, physical, and spiritual liberation) has been transformative, allowing me to share my story with authenticity and strength.

I hope it encourages others to find their own paths to healing.

I've come to understand how Black women often mask pain and trauma, feeling the pressure to appear strong and resilient in the face of adversity. We carry our burdens silently, often at the expense of our well-being. One of the most challenging things that I had to overcome on this journey was feeling like less of a woman after losing my breast. Although externally, no one could identify or recognize that I was without it, I could. During this season, I fell into a deep depression; struggling with vanity rather than being appreciative of life.

Society has set an expectation on outward appearance and if it's not to the "standard," you become a target for malicious intent. I lost my breast, hair, confidence and dignity all in the blink of an eye. What I believed to be a health crisis turned into a death sentence of my physical self. It took me six years to fight my way out of that state of mind. I continued to "motivate" other women through my speaking but was barely scratching the surface of where God wanted me to be. The more I spoke, the more God revealed. Once the scales were completely removed, I realized that my affliction was for good reason. (Psalm 119: 71). I know this sounds crazy; however, once again, it was all working out for my good (Romans 8:28). God was not only using me to set captives free, but he was also FREEING ME! What a relief that was.

Sometimes we get so attached to our struggles that we can't see the good things ahead. There is ALWAYS purpose in the pain.

Believe it. Once I surrendered and embraced my vulnerabilities, real healing took place.

Trauma is designed to keep you down and bound. God wants to FREE US. Don't be afraid to seek pastoral or psychological counseling, as they can both be beneficial and conducted simultaneously. Social determinants, like the mental health stigma, are barriers that can prevent us from getting adequate access to the care we need. The stigma associated is what often prohibits people from embracing the available assistance. Avoidance has exhausted our culture in many ways. As a healthcare professional, I've interviewed several physicians, specifically during the pandemic, who all reported that there was a HUGE uptick in depression. While discussing our feelings might always feel a little awkward, we need to make conversations about mental health more common, so they feel less uncomfortable.

In the depths of my depression, I didn't want to leave home; I couldn't eat; I couldn't mentally bring myself out of it and my outward appearance was suffering as a result. All I would do is cry and wonder why me? Why did I have to be the one that suffered like this? God's response was, "Why NOT you?" In that moment, I knew I was chosen for a time such as this. Every stronghold that had me chained up, must be broken.

Let this testimony help you identify and heal the trauma that has yoked you. Focus on your inner man, so that your outer man can shine bright! As an Ambassador for the American Cancer Society's "Making Strides Against Breast Cancer" across the Southeast Region, I have dedicated my life to bringing awareness and sharing my story on various platforms and environments. I have 23 years of healthcare experience and am fulfilling my purpose in alignment with God's plan. I am an entrepreneur with countless things in store for me to enhance God's Kingdom.

Allow me the opportunity to leave you with some valuable tools. I want you to focus on what it looks like to own your truth and the benefits in your life. I have opened up about my cancer journey with you and shared my truth about feeling like less of a woman during my battle with cancer. The reality for me was that I wanted to free myself from these challenges and fears as it consumed me mentally. Owning your truth means embracing and accepting your authentic self, including your experiences, emotions, and identity, without fear of judgment or rejection.

<u>**What it looks like to own your truth:**</u>

1. <u>**Self-Acceptance**</u>: Embracing all parts of yourself, including your strengths, weaknesses, and past experiences.

2. <u>**Vulnerability**</u>: Being open and honest about your feelings and experiences, even when it feels uncomfortable.

3. **Integrity**: Aligning your actions and decisions with your true values and beliefs.

4. **Confidence:** Feeling secure in who you are and what you stand for, regardless of external validation.

5**. Setting Boundaries**: Knowing your limits and standing firm in them to protect your well-being.

6**. Living Authentically**: Making choices that reflect your true self, rather than conforming to societal expectations.

Now that we know what it looks like to own our truth, let's discuss the benefits of owning your truth:

1. **Mental and Emotional Freedom**: Letting go of the pressure to meet others' expectations can relieve stress and anxiety.

2. **Stronger Relationships**: Authenticity fosters deeper connections with others who appreciate and accept you for who you are.

3. **Personal Growth**: Embracing your truth allows for genuine self-reflection and personal development.

4. **Increased Resilience**: Being true to yourself can build inner strength and help you navigate challenges more effectively.

5. **Empowerment**: Owning your story and experiences can inspire and empower both yourself and others.

6. **Inner Peace**: Living authentically brings a sense of inner harmony and satisfaction.

7. **Greater Fulfillment**: Pursuing goals and passions that resonate with your true self leads to a more fulfilling life.

Owning your truth is a journey that requires courage and self-compassion, but the rewards are profound and far-reaching. I challenge each of you to own your truth. Sometimes it can feel uncomfortable but necessary. Trust me, you've got this.

May the Father God meet you in the areas of your needs and may you be wise enough to allow Him to heal you from the inside out. In the meantime, be on the lookout for my next book, "Provoked to Prevail." Remember, God loves you and so do I.

Blessings,

Rashanda

About the Author

Rashanda is a devoted wife, mother, sister and friend. She has a degree in Medical Billing and has worked in healthcare for 23 years. Rashanda has devoted her time to motivational speaking for the last 12 years. As a health and awareness educator, her professional portfolio is rather extensive. Her passion for writing landed her an opportunity as a contributor and co-writer for "The First Lady Ministry of St. Paul Baptist Church Blog" platform. She was recently named as a model for a luxury t-shirt brand TGS ("Trust God Sis").

Noted for her continuous contributions to the community, Rashanda has been awarded the Presidential Lifetime Achievement Award. She has also been featured in P.O.W.E.R. Magazine, the Times and Democrat, Clay Today, and on FOX35 Orlando news, WLTX News 19 and various radio stations about her community initiatives. She has been a volunteer with the American Cancer Society for six years and was recently named as the Southeastern Region Product Leader for "Making Strides Against Breast Cancer".

She recently ventured into fashion design with her luxury shoe line "The Pink Bottom Company." The first in the collection, PREVAIL, is one of four designs by Mack-Kelly.

Stay tuned for her upcoming book, "Provoked to Prevail."

Connect with me:

Facebook: Rashanda Mack

Instagram: @rashandamk

TikTok: @rashandamack

YouTube: @Shanda_Speaks

Quote and Scripture

"We must work to ensure that every woman has the opportunity to achieve her full health potential, free from social and economic barriers."-Dr. Camara Jones

2 Corinthians 1:4-7-"And the God of all comfort, who comforts us in all our troubles, so that we can comfort those in any trouble with the comfort we ourselves receive from God. For just as we share abundantly in the sufferings of Christ, so also our comfort abounds through Christ. If we are distressed, it is for your comfort and salvation; if we are comforted, it is for your comfort, which produces in you patient endurance of the same sufferings we suffer. And our hope for you is firm, because we know that just as you share in our sufferings, so also you share in our comfort."

Chapter 5: The Black Sheep
By: Calvin Curtis McIntosh

A black sheep in a flock of white ones is considered different and often singled out, but not in a good way. They are deemed as worthless because their wool holds no value. What do black sheep and I have in common? We both struggled to find our place within the flock.

I was born March 27, 1983, to James Wembley and Jennifer McIntosh. I am the middle child of three. As a child, I struggled to find my place within the family. My brother is five years older, and as the first-born child was placed on a pedestal. My sister, one year younger, was the baby girl, and only girl, exalted at every turn. Where did that leave me? The answer is bullied and feeling unloved and unwanted!

I come from home filled with love from broken people. My mother was a hardworking woman. My father had a troubled childhood that shaped him as a man. As a father, he was loving and compassionate, but not always available when we wanted him. When he was around, he always embraced us, showered us with his love, and poured into us.

I grew up in the church. My grandmother was a pastor, making my mother was a PK (Pastor's Kid) who also served as the choir director. Being in church everyday showed me a way to live life. Outside the church showed me a darker side. I would love to say that I chose the lighter way, but life circumstances ensnared me to the dark.

Being born in the 80's and growing up in the 90's, drugs and alcohol were prevalent in my upbringing.

Living in the hood and seeing my father, uncles, and cousins use both made it normal for me. These vices kept my father away for days or weeks at a time. Without a male influence, I had to fend for myself at the tender age of 4 years old.

As a husky child, it should have been easier for me to defend myself, but instead, my physique seemed to incite the bullying. When my older brother should have been the person to protect and defend me, he instead became my tormentor. Where his terrorizing ended, my younger sister's began. They were merciless, to the point I contemplated suicide at age 5... This was just the beginning of my childhood trauma.

While it is hard to imagine that more trauma would come from my family, but it did. My mom was now a hard-working single parent, raising three children, who could not always find a babysitter or daycare for us. Therefore, babysitting duties usually fell to my extended family, specifically, my cousins. Until much later in life, I never told anyone that one of those babysitters touched and molested me when I was young. This violation planted the seed of sexual carnality in my mind; one too young to understand the gravity of the situation.

As a child of the 80's, VHS tapes and "dirty" magazines were popular and readily available to me because I had older brothers and cousins. Being around women at house parties enhanced my sexual desires.

Lustful wantonness grew through with every exposure, all of which left me misunderstanding how a woman should be treated.

I became a product of my environment, living in the hood, surrounded by gangs and violence. My dad exposed me to drugs; I tasted alcohol when I was still in diapers. Food stamps helped provide for our needs. The house parties, "dirty" movies and magazines showed that women were tools used to satisfy needs, which led me to become a womanizer later in life. Being molested introduced me to person-to-person sex. The overexposure was tremendous, my grades were even affected, and these behaviors became normal to me. So normal, that I did not realize how dysfunctional it was or how much trauma was inflicted on me.

As disturbing as this part of my childhood was, it was not the most traumatic. An event when I was twelve changed everything for me. My mom, brother, sister, and I were shopping in a store, when she told us we could get a toy... I was so excited. As we exited the store, the only thing I remember was going through the door and hearing my brother and sister screaming as they turned toward me. I was on the concrete shaking vigorously with an uncontrollable seizure; the first of many. Doctors determined this was an epileptic seizure but could not pinpoint the cause.

I was frustrated and confused as to what caused the seizure, which was only compounded by the often-compassionless environment that is high school.

High school is hard enough without being viewed as an outcast and labeled a freak. As the seizures returned, so did the ridicule, mockery and cruelty from my high school classmates, who would stare, point, and laugh at me. No one offered to help or checked on me after an episode. I often wondered if they would still be laughing had I died from the seizure. Thankfully, we will never know that answer.

The relentless torment from my seizures triggered me back to my childhood. I still vividly remembered my siblings bullying me. I felt useless, unloved, and unwanted then and again, in that moment. Because I never addressed my childhood trauma, the high school bullying affected me on a deeper level. Even though I was older, I was still too immature to understand that a medical issue caused these episodes. Instead, I felt abnormal. The pressure of being a teenager and trying to find my identity was compounded by my addictions to alcohol, drugs and sex.

My new normal became a compilation of all the vices I had, plus seizures, and the medications that were dispensed to try and regulate their effects. I detested going to the doctor because they only had ominous predictions for my life. They focused on what I would never be able to do: drive, live a normal life, or have children. Their advice was to file for disability and collect the check. They essentially handed me a death sentence!

This black sheep was determined to stand out for doing what the doctor's deemed impossible. In the face of this adversity, I chose to live! I graduated high school and even walked down the aisle and onto the stage to receive my diploma. I obtained my driver's license and drove myself to nursing school. I was the only sibling to graduate high school and further my education.

The doctor's told me I would not live a normal life, but what they failed to understand was that my life wasn't normal anyway. I buried my trauma and anguish deep; never speaking to anyone about it. Who would have believed the words of a young child? I had even convinced myself that this trauma didn't affect my life. Yet, I could not lie about my overwhelming need to be wanted and loved unconditionally.

This need was ingrained in me since early in my childhood. My experiences with love and affection came from a father who would come home drunk or high and profess his love for us. He would hug and kiss us and say I love you. He emphasized how much he loved us despite his imperfections and absenteeism. His unhealthy behavior laid the foundation for a parent-child relationship. It also left me hungry for love and determined that I would be different as a father.

My mindset was put to the test when I was nineteen, when I discovered that I was going to be a dad!

The child's paternity was in question; deep in my heart I knew I was not the father. Even though I was young, I was determined to be the child's dad. The deepest recesses of my heart screamed that this was my chance to receive the unconditional love I longed for my entire life! Like my father, I had my own flaws and imperfections. Yet I was determined to remain a steady presence in my child's life. This was my chance to break the fatherhood mold my dad established! This child would be the healing balm to the trauma I experienced as a child. He or she could fill the holes of my heart and help motivate me to strive to be a better person!

I wanted so badly to be more than what I appeared from the life I was dealt. But I was a child raising a child. There was no parenting instruction manual. I was young and immature. I continued to feed my alcohol, drugs and sex addictions while dealing with baby mama drama. I did not know how to parent, but I was trying.

I loved that child as if she were my own. And while deep in my heart I knew she was not mine; my heart was ripped to shreds when I received confirmation. When I saw those test results, I was hurt and cried uncontrollably. However, I loved her too much to walk away. I was not willing to let my only chance for unconditional love slip through my fingers. This child needed a father, and I needed someone to love, as much as I needed someone to love me!

Years passed and I finally met someone that I believed was the one for me. You know, the one that you are destined to love and be with for the rest of your life. This was my first "real" relationship, and I was determined it would be my last. However, the affects of unaddressed trauma began to pollute the relationship. The weight of the abandonment, bullying, hurt, molestation and want to be loved suffocated us. I loved her and she loved me, but our love was not enough to overcome the deeply buried trauma effects. The words "I Love You" easily left my lips. Yet the unspoken truths from my childhood stuck in my throat and refused to be moved! When will I ever find the courage or place to unbury this pain and free myself from the trauma bondage?

What we bury deep will eventually find its way to the surface. To be more exact, God will guide us to a place or person to speak of our "dirty little secrets" that are eating away at our soul. This was true for me when I attended a men's revival at a local church. A man arose from the crowd. I was shocked by the words he spoke. He told of being molested as a child by his sibling. To my surprise, others told their molestation stories too. My spirit was overcome with a desperate need to be free. It felt as if my body were on fire trying to burn the chains of my childhood trauma. My blood flowed with power and my heart pumped with courage, as I rose from my chair. With just a mustard seed of faith, the words buried deep in my soul flew from my lips as I recounted my molestation experience.

This was the first time I shared my story. I did not realize my brother was sitting behind me until I heard him gasp when I stood up. He never knew what happened and was shocked hearing my testimony. He fervently told me that our parents needed to know this too! I was apprehensive but agreed to tell them.

We went to my parent's house, where my brother gathered the family and said, "Calvin has something he needs to tell all of you." I stood there staring at them, wondering how do I tell my family this news? How will they respond? Will their response help disperse the shame and pain or add to it?

I took a deep breath and with a trembling voice recounted my experience. "Remember when I was a child, and you used to drop us off at the babysitter? Well, that babysitter took advantage of me and did things to me that a babysitter should not do to a child." I finished my story, anxiously awaiting their reactions, unsure and fearing how they would respond.

I was flabbergasted by their reactions and how much my parents had changed since my youth. My father went to rehab and got clean. He worked hard to have a steady good-paying job, create a new life and become a better man. Our relationship was healthy and the best it had ever been. He burst into tears and held me, then got angry and wanted to find and kill this family member!

My mother's reaction was quite the opposite. She looked at me with a straight face and said, "Wow, at least you did not turn out like most men or people who have been molested." I was speechless and stood staring at her. I exclaimed, "What do you mean?" With little emotion, she responded, "Most people that were molested, especially men, grow up to molest children or become rapists." Not only were the words she spoke appalling but so was her lack of emotion or compassion. Instead of a loving and caring motherly response, I was left with her statement that at least I did not become a child molester! What mother

says that kind of things to her son? Definitely not the responses I expected from them.

My mind raced with thoughts after her "speech," but my mouth stayed shut. I wanted to scream at her that... no, I did not grow up to be a child molester or a rapist, instead, I was a child who was violated and became addicted to sex, drugs, and alcohol. At the time of my assault, I was too young to understand what sex was or how to use those body parts. Because of this, I thought it was normal for a child to take advantage of another child. Leave it to my mother to state that that experience did not make me a pedophile. My childhood exposure to alcohol, drugs, and sex was a breeding ground for pedophile behavior! According to my mom's comment, I should be thankful that I only became a manipulated child with addictive vice... And be thankful that I did not become a rapist, instead I only mistreated women in non-violent ways.

Are you serious? My childhood had lasting effects long into my adult life. Here I am sharing with you a traumatic experience, and this is how you react! Mothers are supposed to be comforters. Now the roles were reversed, and my father was the parent providing support and comfort.

I wanted to tell my parents so I could finally release the weight of this event and start to heal. However, telling them made it worse. In this extremely vulnerable moment, all I wanted was to feel heard and know that I was loved regardless. At least my father expressed his love and did what he could to comfort me. If those reactions weren't shocking enough, my perpetrator was still invited to family events: anniversaries, birthday parties, and even to my father's funeral! To say that upset me is a mild understatement! At least the person avoided talking to me. On the rare occasions that we interacted, I saw in their eyes that they knew I finally understood what they did to me.

My family's response to my experience was disheartening. I understand why people don't speak about their trauma; why they hold it in even at great cost to their body and mind. I truly was the black sheep of my family - away from the herd and left to fend for myself! I finally mustered up enough courage to tell them and the end result was another layer added to the hurt and pain. This time, I felt abandoned by my mother... What a change from my childhood!

I was accustomed to my father expressing his love for me, but my mother never said she loved me until I was

in my thirties. I told her that was all I wanted to hear when I lost my tooth, skinned my knee, or was growing up as a teenager in a difficult environment. Then I expressed how my deep-rooted need to feel loved influenced not only my choices but also my life. She hugged me and whispered her words of love. Her actions should have been comforting, but I just felt uncomfortable. Not trying to compare my parents, but with dad love expressions made me feel secure. No matter if we were sitting and watching television, dad would find us, grab us, and kiss our cheeks. My heart expanded even if I never admitted it to him. It was those memories of him showing me love that led me to forgive him for not being the father I needed him to be. How I miss those kisses and expressions of love now that he is gone. As I reflect on my childhood, I can see that my dad did his best to feed my insatiable need to be loved.

The doctors told me I would never live a normal life. My childhood showed me that normal is what you make it to be. My belief for a long time was that you are a product of your environment. Now, I can see that your circumstances and how you respond to them shape your character. The weight from your trauma can bring you to your knees. This posture was where God showed me the truths from my trauma-filled life. The truth is despite what I experienced in life and what was stolen from my childhood, I am still standing!

I AM STILL STANDING DESPITE BEING:

• Addicted to alcohol, drugs, and sex

• Diagnosed with epilepsy without a cure

   • Told that I could never drive (I proved the doctors wrong)

• Violated by someone in the worst way

• Never feeling loved or wanted

• Losing my father (my best friend)

• In failed relationships; coupled with the pain of discovering a child I loved was not mine

You often hear that God will take your mess and turn it into your message for His kingdom. I am living proof of the truth in this statement. We are hesitant to be vulnerable in our brokenness because we do not fully understand the power that lies in our testimonies for God.

As I discuss my failures from my past, I can also joyously declare the blessings in my life now. I have a beautiful wife and children, own my home, have multiple businesses, travel the world, and do not allow my epilepsy to control my life! God brought peace to my past. As I deepened my relationship with Him, I found the unconditional love I always craved. He loves every part of me, the ugly and beautiful parts!

My experience with epilepsy and childhood molestation gives me insight to help others understand and navigate through the setbacks both can have on your life. I stand tall and proclaim how my past shaped my life. My traumatic history is the framework to show how God's grace can heal our deepest wounds and inflictions. God's grace, not my own power or will, led me to find a platform to reach other men to help release them from their own bondage.

Now, I no longer struggle to find my place within the flock. I have embraced being the black sheep. The value of the black sheep is not determined by its wool. Instead, the value is found in the ability to stand out in a crowd of many. I am unique and different from the rest. I learned to embrace my flaws and imperfections because they make me relatable. The experiences I had in life can be used as teachable moments for others. I thought my life was over, but it was just the beginning chapter of my life story! I am the black sheep and despite all that life dealt me, I am still standing! More importantly, I'm standing in the knowledge that God can use me for a greater purpose and my need for unconditional love has been fulfilled!

About the Author

Calvin Curtis McIntosh was born and raised in Akron, Ohio. He graduated from John R Buchtel. Calvin is married to Tiffany McIntosh and a father to two beautiful girls ShaeAuna Stevens and Aniyah McIntosh.

Having epilepsy hasn't stopped Calvin from pursuing his dream of becoming an entrepreneur. He is an example to everyone that having a life-altering illness doesn't have to keep you from achieving your goals and dreams!

Follow Me:

Facebook: CalvinMcIntosh

Instagram: @Calicalmac83

TikTok: Calicalmac1

Quote and Scripture

If nothing changes, nothing changes.-Courtney C. Stevens

John 14:27-"Peace I leave with you; my peace I give you. I do not give to you as the world gives. Do not let your hearts be troubled and do not be afraid."

Chapter 6: The Silent Struggle: Living Through and Beyond Abuse
By: Shavonne Renee

After a ten-year relationship enthralled with domestic violence, which comes to the forefront frequently, I often question my mindset and mental health during that period. For much of that time I thought that I was happy. I was not. I was fearful, ashamed, and just going along to get along. I was not raised in an abusive environment or led to believe I had to accept that lifestyle. I grew up in a loving home with both of my parents, happily married. They had arguments and disagreements, but who doesn't? They loved each other, and they stuck it out through all the rough times. I felt like that was the goal; to find a companion and make it work, through thick and thin. I took the thin a little too literally.

What I thought was true love started in my freshman year of high school. We are going to call my true love Skip. He was just a regular guy, nothing exciting about him. He was not a sports jock or the most popular guy in school, but Skip was charming. He had a way of instantly making me feel like I was the only girl in the world. I remember when we officially met, he approached me and offered to walk me to class. We ate lunch together every day and he walked me to class as often as possible, always carrying my books. We did not talk much outside of school. Skip was horrified of my father, who was strict about phone use and everything else. My siblings and I were very sheltered children. We were allowed two hours a day, two days a week split between the three of us.

After a few months, Skip began to ignore me at school, walking past me as if I were invisible.

I felt non-existent; completely crushed. When I finally got his attention to ask what happened, he claimed someone told him I was cheating. The catalyst told him that I was spending my nights up late on the phone with another boy. Now, when I was in high school, talking on the phone with someone else was seriously a big deal! However, based on my father's rules, he knew this could not be true, but he needed a way out because he had his sights on someone else. By the end of the day, he was walking another girl to class. My heart was shattered. Love, as I knew it, was the most painful thing that I had ever experienced. I was confused and angry. How dare he accuse me of cheating and take someone else's word over mine. I did not realize at the time that this was a classic narcissistic move: make me the bad guy so he would not feel guilty. We barely spoke after that; a little in passing. One day, I was walking outside during lunch period with a few of my friends. He grabbed my hand and stopped me. He told me how much he loved me and missed hanging out with me. It really touched me, and I got very emotional. I wasn't sure why I was crying. Certainly, I could not have had feelings for him that strong, but I did. The rush of emotions just made me feel as though it was a natural attraction, and we were supposed to make our way back together. I thought Skip and I felt the same way. I believed in my heart that we were going to be high school sweethearts like my parents were. We began talking again, nothing consistent, but I thought that we were headed to a good place. The summer after our junior year, he had his first child, and I was crushed all over again.

The way I understood mutual love, he was not supposed to be out being intimate with anyone else. This is something that he and I had yet to speak about, and I just assumed that he was not speaking to anyone else about it either. Physically, I felt sick. My appetite was almost non-existent, and I just had no desire to talk to anyone. My mother knew something was bothering me, but I could never bring myself to tell her what was going on.

Halfway through senior year, Skip was expelled from school. He still had my number, so we talked here and there, increasing to almost every night after my graduation. One night, during my freshman year in college, he called when I was at a sorority probate show. I stepped out of the event to tell him I would call back once I returned to my dorm. He was highly dissatisfied that I prioritized anything over talking to him and had no problem letting me know as much. He yelled, cursed, and accused me of not caring about him. That was the last time we spoke for another three years. This time, I was not upset. I honestly didn't feel anything but confusion.

When we reconnected, he was not all that impressive, but all the feelings that I thought were gone came rushing back. I began feeling like that girl in high school being walked to class. He had a job, but it was not what some might call a decent job. He had another child since we last spoke. As an extremely sheltered child, I had very few interactions with people outside of family and school. I honestly had no idea what to look for in a relationship outside of what my parents had built; meet your soulmate in high school, get married, have kids, and take the bad with the good. So, when he came back around and was still showing me the same attention that he used to, as if no time had passed, I was stuck. There is an old saying "If you love something you have to let it go, and if it comes back, then it is meant to be." Well, he came back, so he must have been the person that was meant for me. I was always so captivated by him calling me his high school sweetheart. I thought that it really meant something because that is the love story that I grew up watching with my parents. Subconsciously, I really was trying to recreate their life. Most people I know long for that happily ever after.

Shortly after we began hanging out, things escalated between us quickly. I found myself pregnant within a few months, and all I could do was cry. I was in my junior year of college, majoring in accounting. How was I going to finish with a baby? This is not a part of the plan that I had laid out for myself. I was supposed to be a college graduate and married before I had my first child. I was so afraid to tell my father, so I asked my mom to deliver the news. My dad was always very stern and strict. My siblings and I jokingly called him the drill sergeant behind his back. Well into adulthood, I was scared to break any rules because there was always the possibility that he would find out. For all I knew, he might still try to spank me, although I would hope not. My father, knowing my introverted and quiet nature, refused to believe I was pregnant until he held his first grandchild.

Once he realized the type of man I was stuck with, he began to change how he dealt with me. I was about 8 months pregnant when the first serious attack happened. Skip and I were talking about where I would live once I gave birth. We both still lived at home with our parents at the time, so the options really carried the same weight. I told him that for the first week or two, I would like to be home with my own mother, and not with his. I really felt like this was a time that I needed to be close to my mom and really embrace motherhood, learning from her like I had done my entire life. This did not mean that he was not welcomed to visit and stay awhile with me and our baby, but that was exactly how he took it. He immediately began accusing me of trying to take the baby from him and not allowing him to be a father. Somewhere in the middle of him assaulting me, his brother came home from school. We did not know that he was in the house until I was able to break free and run outside, where the assault continued. I was able to drive off, to the next street over where the lady that I knew called my father, who brought the police with him. They took pictures of my bruises and scratches. They also took pictures of my braids on the ground that he had pulled out and my bloody handprints down the side of the car where he kept dragging me back whenever I tried to get inside. His brother, who caught the end of the altercation gave a statement to the police saying that he never touched me and that he was just trying to stop me from beating his son with a coffee mug.

We lived in a small county, where everybody knew everybody.

The police and EMS that responded to the scene were people that I had graduated high school with. I was so embarrassed to let anyone know what I had gone through. When I went to my parents with the next altercation, they did not offer any assistance, advice, or empathy. My dad turned cold towards me. He did not call as often. He removed me from his car insurance and took out a life insurance policy on me and my child, convinced this man would kill us.

When my father first informed me about the insurance policy, I was offended for quite some time, but I never told him. Did he not trust my judgement? Did he think I would let things get that far? Now that I am out of that unfortunate environment, I fully understand why he did what he did. He knew I had to learn the lesson on my own, but he did not know whether I would learn too late. I clearly had no control over the situation no matter how composed I tried to appear. I tried hard to hide the abuse and my unhappiness, but it was written all over my face. My spirit was broken. The eruptions started subtly, with name-calling and belittling, triggered by anything, from not wanting to cook to not letting him use my car. The emotional abuse and manipulation, I believe, was so much worse than the physical, at times. The physical scars would heal. The emotional damage is still being hauled around to this day. At first the abuse was never noticeable to others.

He would hit me on the head, so my hair would hide the knots. Another one of the first physical altercations I recall was when I was a few months pregnant. He asked if I was in love with him, and I said no. I did love him, but I was not in love. I had not had the time or peace to fall in love. I became pregnant so quickly, and everything was a snowball effect after that. There was always panic or a fight if I did not go along with every little thing that he said or wanted me to do. I do not think I was ever in love. Early on, it was the infatuation of being high school sweethearts living happily ever after. Then it just became a part of my life that I got used to. He was livid, as if that were going to change my feelings.

Domestic violence, while pregnant, is the single most miserable situation I have ever experienced. I was so stressed that I began to lose weight at an alarming rate. After delivery, I weighed less than I did in high school. The baby was healthy, so my doctor was not too concerned but still warned me to leave. She suspected the abuse from our first meeting. She asked him to leave the room and directly asked me if I was being abused. She could tell from our initial conversation and his vibe alone. Of course, I lied, but she knew better. I can imagine being in her profession, she sees a lot and can easily identify the signs.

The physical abuse intensified quickly. My supervisors at work often tried to cover my black eyes with makeup, and coworkers wrapped my hair where he had pulled out my braids. I lost a few jobs because I had to call out, being that I was too sore and unable to move some

days. Every day, someone lectured me about knowing when it was time to leave, from the doctor treating my wounds at the emergency room to the responding officers after another incident. "Shavonne, when will you be tired? Shavonne, when will you stop? Shavonne, when will you have enough?" The level of embarrassment I felt remains unmatched. In my mind, I knew that I had enough. I knew I was tired and wanted no parts of this man. But we had a child together, so I felt like I had to make it work. Maybe if I loved him enough, he would change.

By the time I was fighting through my second pregnancy, I was exhausted. I began to beat him to the madness, feeling the anger transfer from him to me. I thought it would not be as bad if I did not let him catch me off guard, but this gave him the ammunition to play the victim and paint me as the aggressor. It did not take long for me to become mentally drained. A man who did not love me was in my house, refusing to leave. Whenever he did leave, he was gone for days, sometimes weeks. Unexpectedly, he would return to see the kids and just never leave. There was some fear inside of me. I am still confused about what type of fear I had. If someone would ask me if I was afraid of him, I would always respond with a stern absolutely not, and I meant that! I was not scared of him, but the situation. I would get mixed advice from different officers and of course my trusted internet searches. Some would read that if he assaulted me and I fought back, we both would be arrested for mutual combat. What would happen to my kids?

At some point, I stopped reporting because he would always return, and I was back in the hamster wheel of a cycle. I soon discovered that it was easier to just go along to get along. "You want my car? Take it. Do you want my phone? Take it." I was miserable, but it made my life easier until I could find a way out.

A friend lectured me about leaving. I heard her, but it was not that simple. I often tried to downplay the entire situation as though it was not as serious as she was making out to be. One day, she came to visit and meet the new baby. We thought that he had left but turns out he was standing outside the front door listening to everything we were discussing. She called her husband to check in, and he thought that she was calling a man for me to meet. He burst into the front door in such a rage! She saw firsthand what she had heard on the phone so many times before. She told me she could no longer be my friend because she refused to watch me die, if it ever went that far. I respected her decision but resented her for it. She was supposed to be my friend, to have my back, to help me. I needed help and support, even if it was just emotional. I was already so lost and broken and her leaving me just intensified all those feelings.

As I got older and gained more life experience, I understood her decision more. What could she do for me that I could not do for myself? She could not make me leave. Every conversation had a new situation, which must have been emotionally tiring for her. She was my friend when she could be.

When I told her he took my car without permission, she offered to take me to get it. When I called her crying, she offered her place for me and my daughter to stay. She did what she could until she could not. I appreciate her now more than ever.

He never outright said it, but I am certain he loved that I was losing friends and family. When I told him I was going to a family function or out with a friend, it always caused a blow-up. He would call repeatedly, send offensive and vulgar texts, and post horrible things about me on social media. At first, I felt the need to argue and tell my side. Eventually, I blocked him because I looked just as foolish as he did. I felt foolish. I knew that I was not doing the things that he was accusing me of, but my side had to be told. I thought that if he said it then of course people would believe it. Blocking him was good for my peace, but this caused another problem. He felt other men had access to me on social media when he did not. He felt this way because he used these platforms as a dating service. He had many relationships during and after ours but still made my life miserable. Stalking, threatening my life, and reporting false claims to social services were his tactics. Even after I moved, the unannounced and uninvited pop-ups were ridiculous. In the aftermath, I was diagnosed with PTSD and struggled mentally.

Sometimes, I felt he behaved this way because he was unsatisfied with his life. I often tried to help him make changes to get ahead. It is true what they say: you cannot help someone who is not willing to change.

I found GED classes for him, but he accused me of being a snake and not genuinely wanting to help. When he finally enrolled, he was upset that I would not do the homework for him. I was working two jobs and in college myself; there was no way I had time to work, be a mother, do his homework, and mine too. I suggested family therapy as something we could do together, but he refused, feeling he had no problems and everyone else did.

The road to rebuilding myself was one I never expected to travel because I never thought that I would be broken in such a way. I never thought I would co-parent with someone who had me covered in bruises. I never imagined I would have to co-parent at all. I grew up in a two-parent household and tried with everything I could to provide the same for my children. The process is ongoing and triple hard with two kids who need healing as well. I must be strong for them and rebuild myself on the backend.

My children have different perspectives of their dad. One witnessed much of the abuse and was subject to mental and emotional abuse directly. This child chooses not to engage with him, and he feels I should force it. I left my children exposed to abuse for so long. At some point, I had to be their mother and advocate. My child tried more than once to explain their feelings to him. He responded by getting irate, using profane language, and saying children have no right to feel that way. I decided that it was the last time they would have that discussion. It was too painful for a child and left me with questions I could not answer and pieces I could not put back together.

My other child is not old enough to remember the fits and episodes and loves their dad. I love that for this child, but it puts me in a difficult position when he wants to pop up and engage with his children. Therapy taught me to always give them the choice. They are old enough, and their feelings are valid. I am doing what I feel is best for them every day. Every day I pray that I am not causing further damage to them. I talk to my children and encourage them to be as open as possible and come to me with any and everything that they are feeling. I do not ever want them to feel like they must take sides or say what they think I want to hear.

Watching the abuse led my oldest to be overprotective of me. If I ran into a guy friend in the street and said hello, my child was asking who that was and stated that it should only be me and the two of them. We did not need anyone else. I did my best to never put them in a situation where they needed to choose sides between me and their father, but sometimes he made it impossible. He would want to see the kids, but it may have been a day where they just did not want to see them, and I would advise him of that. He would respond with I was filling their heads with terrible things about him and that I was telling them that I did not want them to see him. That was not the case at all. They witnessed so much, and they did love their father through it all, but some days they just did not want to interact with him because they did not know what type of mood he would be in that day.

When he did not believe me, he would ask them directly and I did not like that.

It made me feel as though he was deliberately trying to put them in between our mess. When he was mad at me and decided to disappear, he would disappear on the kids as well. He would not call to check on them or anything. My heart used to break so badly for them. My relationship with him should not have had any effect on his relationship with the kids, but to him, they were one in the same.

Now that I am out, it is so much easier to pursue my dreams and appreciate every step without him demeaning my accomplishments. I remember when I would get a promotion at work and was so excited to tell him. He would respond saying that the promotion better stay at work because I was not the supervisor of anything outside of work. I had gotten so used to never being celebrated that sometimes, I still second-guess myself and wonder if I am worthy of all I desire. If I am not, I am certain my children are. This is a mistake many of us make. We want to give the world to our children, but everything cannot be about them. We must put ourselves first to be the best we can be for them. At some point, they will grow up and go out on their own. What will we be working for then if we make them our "why" for everything? We must be our own "why." We must participate in our own rescue. I know I hold the power to control my life, and it is well beyond time I took that power back.

About the Author

Shavonne Prescott is an entrepreneur, aspiring author, and advocate for joy, inspiration, and beauty in every facet of life. As the proud owner of Gracious Jade Services and Captured Journeys, she empowers others through photography and officiating weddings. She demonstrates many ways to own your life.

Shavonne also dedicates her free time to honing and mastering her craft. She indulges in reading and cherishes vacations, especially by the water.

Mothering two brilliant children, she recently relocated to her hometown in South Carolina for a fresh start, harnessing clarity, and determination.

Her diverse career spans food, retail, law enforcement, and medical sectors—each opportunity allowing her to positively impact countless lives. Shavonne's passion lies in motivating and inspiring others, a calling she now pursues on her terms and timeline.

Writing has been her lifelong passion, alongside capturing moments of profound beauty through photography. Despite a decade-long domestic violence ordeal that robbed her of motivation and inspiration, Shavonne emerged stronger and with more determination than ever before. Shifting her focus from her losses, she began to appreciate all that she had gained.

Today, Shavonne is reclaiming her voice and vision. Through her work and words, she strives to showcase life's enduring beauty and resilience. It is about seizing opportunities and embracing the power within to create a life filled with purpose and positivity.

Connect with me:

Facebook:Shavonne Prescott

Instagram:@iam_shavonne

Linked In: Shavonne Prescott

Snapchat: iam-shavonne

Twitter: i_amshavonne

Quote and Scripture

"We may encounter many defeats, but we must not be defeated." - Maya Angelou

Psalm 72:14-"He will rescue them from oppression and violence, for precious is their blood in his sight."

Chapter 7: The Beating Stopped on March 18th

By: TanTisha Mitchell

March 18, 2004. Before I went to bed that night, I had no idea that would be the day God set me free. Imagine trying to figure out if you are having a bad dream or are you waking up to a miscarriage. As my eyes opened, I realize that it was actual reality and a miscarriage I wasn't having, but instead my ex-husband Ricky was beating me with a fan in his hand; hitting me on multiple parts of my body. Instinctively I was protecting my stomach, as I found out I was six weeks pregnant before I went to sleep that night.

I called out for my sister, who had been staying with us, unaware she had already left for her court appointment. Her presence in our home had deterred much of the physical abuse to which I was accustomed. Regardless, I was still confused about what was going on and what led to all these body blows I was receiving. The only thing I could do was protect my stomach and just scream because the pain was so unbearable. I was convinced that if I could find the strength to get up, that it was either going to be me or him. Already a mother to a four year old, I started having flashbacks of some of the assaults that I had to endure: him pinning me in a corner surrounded by vicious dogs; spraying me down with a water hose, as if I wasn't a human; when he chased me to the police station and jumped on me; then the time when he stabbed me in my leg, forcing me to run down a very busy street with my son screaming and crying for help; along with all the times I went to the hospital where I remember hearing the doctor's voice saying to me "there might not be a next time." Suddenly, I was back in my childhood recalling my mother and father arguing and my mother brandishing a knife.

I knew in that moment that my sister's worst fear would soon be a reality: having to identify my body or his family identifying his. Before I could make my escape to the kitchen to get a knife, I heard a loud knock on the door. "TEMPLE POLICE - OPEN UP!" I could see shadows by my window since I live in a bottom floor apartment. The police had the apartment surrounded, so Ricky jumping out the window [or any other escape route] wasn't an option. I think he was hiding in the bathroom. Shaking uncontrollably and in quite a bit of pain, I tried to get to the door and calm myself down.

I scrambled around trying to grab all the drugs that were in plain sight. While trying to escape, Ricky may have stepped on some that were on the carpet. Then I heard them again: "TEMPLE POLICE - OPEN UP!" By this time, I knew they could see my silhouette. I had tried to clean up without making noise, but didn't have time to grab a vacuum, so the only thing I could do was lay a blanket and a pillow down, as if someone had slept there. Aware of an existing restraining order they were now threatening to kick in the door.

I yelled out "hold on. I don't have any clothes on. Let me get dressed." I was terrified and tried to act confused about why they were there, while hiding the evidence of the assault. When I opened the door, I acted as if I had been sleeping. The police asked me for my name and date of birth. Not having a reason to lie, I replied "TanTisha Adams, 05/03/81." They rushed right in that house, found him hiding in the bathroom and brought him back out in handcuffs.

While I tried to clear any visible paraphernalia, I hadn't realized Ricky had rolled up some marijuana and left residue on the table; probably enough for somebody to have rolled a joint. A friend came to take my son out of the apartment, but in the chaos, I forgot to grab a blue bag of narcotics hidden in a basket of clean clothes. I didn't think the police would want to search the house for anything other than him. When they asked if they could search the house, he said no and told them to ask me. I refused, suggesting they get a search warrant. Dallas, an officer who had been targeting me for a while, arrived. I was already out on bond for possession of a controlled substance - I am certain he had planted crack cocaine in my vehicle during a previous stop. Officer Dallas came in, started kicking things around, and discovered crack cocaine on the floor. He looked at me and said, "Miss Boykins (this officer knew me by my maiden name) you're on your way to Waco after the EMTs take you to the hospital to check you out."

They took me to the hospital in an ambulance, where I spent an hour or two thinking about how I was on my way to the federal jail. Looking at the alternative, had the police not intervened, I was grateful I would be out one day to see my son and the baby I was carrying. The doctor who seemed to be present every time I came in, walked in with the police officer and said, "This is your lucky day - your husband took ownership for all the drugs that we found in the house. After were done evaluating you, you are free to go." That was the first time I felt a sense of relief. I laid back in bed and cried, overwhelmed by the weight of everything that had happened.

I had reached a point where it was either me or him. Reflecting on my previous relationship, I had used a knife in a desperate attempt to defend myself before, but with him, in this case, I felt trapped. I knew that if I stabbed him, it would mean killing him. It would have been a bloodbath - one of those horrific scenes you read about where someone is stabbed over a hundred times. I constantly prayed to God to remove him from my life before that could happen. I had my son and a pregnancy to live for, and I was exhausted - physically, mentally, and emotionally. I believe wholeheartedly that it was a God thing that the police came when they did. Had they not come, I might not be here writing this.

Ricky felt it was his responsibility to help me because I was also involved with drugs, so he ended up going to jail. Having never been in trouble beyond juvenile issues and misdemeanors, had he kept his hands to himself, the police wouldn't have been called, and he wouldn't have faced such severe charges. With his record, they were determined to make an example of him. Because he prevented me from being imprisoned, I told the district attorney I thought he had stabbed me, but later realized the blood on the fence was from when I tried to jump. The state dropped the charge of assault with a deadly weapon and Ricky received time and was sent to a federal prison in Texas.

He had plans to kill me upon release from prison. The only reason he didn't act immediately was that he knew he would be the number one suspect. We went our separate ways, but since he missed so much time with his son, I allowed him to spend time with him when he got out. He once told me that the only way I could leave him was if I died. Fortunately, Ricky went back to prison, where he couldn't act on his threats. I still had so much anger and hatred inside me.

73

Then, in 2016, God woke me up and told me that He couldn't help me until I forgave Ricky. I was instructed to drive three hours to the prison to tell him I forgave him. Despite the long drive and the brief visitation time, I obeyed. When I saw him, he looked me in the eyes and apologized. For the first time, I saw genuine remorse from him. I told him I forgave him - not just for the abuse, but also for the damage to my daughter's clothing. (This daughter was from a previous relationship). He grabbed the outfit she died wearing from the closet and poured paint over it. Even more appalling, Ricky threatened to burn my daughter's grave!

I became a product of my environment. The emotional and mental abuse I suffered led me to become the abuser in my future relationships with men. I later learned that this was my trauma response from the abuse I suffered. God knew I needed to heal from this, and He promised that He would handle the rest if I took this step.

Over the years, Ricky and I became somewhat closer. He would share stories with me, and I found myself reflecting on them with a mix of emotions. Before I started writing this chapter, we experienced a traumatic family event that drew us closer to each other. God said it was time to write about it to help others find freedom. I sent Ricky a message asking him to call me. When he did, I told him I was writing a book. He was excited at first, thinking it was related to what had brought us closer together. I told him no - it was about him, titled "Surviving Ricky." He laughed, thinking I was joking, but when he realized I was serious, he initially asked me not to do it. I insisted that I had to. Then he asked me, "Tisha was I really that bad?" And I replied, "The worst." But I told him I was letting God get the glory out of it, and I thanked him for giving me a story to write. Without his actions, I wouldn't have been able to help others, so I dedicate this book to the person who caused my pain. Thank you, because that pain became my purpose. There were countless days and untold stories I left out, and no one knows how I used to cry myself to sleep, uncertain if I would wake up. I would lie awake watching him sleep so peacefully, wondering how he could rest so comfortably after all he had done to me. Once a man named Chris simply raised his hand to gesture, and I flinched and covered my face. Seeing my reaction brought tears to his eyes, as he realized I was a victim of domestic violence. He hugged me and kept apologizing, even though he wasn't the one who had hurt me. It felt as though God was using him to wrap His arms around me through a physical embrace. Although this is just a glimpse of the book, it still holds a significant amount of enlightenment on how being abused can influence lives in different ways.

About the Author

TanTisha Mitchell is a wife, mother to nine, and grandmother to one. She has a big heart for helping others, with a soft spot for saving troubled teens. Born in Temple, Texas as an "Army brat," TanTisha moved to Germany after birth because of her father's military career. Much of her childhood was spent traveling the world, which she very much enjoyed and can say influenced her greatly.

After the parting of her first marriage, she returned to a familiar life, becoming a military wife. After her husband's retirement, they moved back to Texas. She became an entrepreneur and opened up Mitchell & Blessed Freight. Ancestry DNA and connecting families are her passions.

TanTisha currently resides in Houston, Texas. Current projects include finalizing her nonprofit and writing another book.

Connect with me:

Facebook: TanTisha Mitchell

Instagram: @starrzshinebright and @blessingsandgifts81

TikTok: @tantishamitchell

Quote and Scripture

You've got to learn to leave the table when love's no longer being served.-Nina Simone

Exodus 3:14-"God said to Moses, "I AM WHO I AM. This is what you are to say to the Israelites: I am has sent me to you.""

Chapter 8: Surviving and Thriving after Breast Cancer

By: Dr. C. Renee Coleman

Woman Problems

On the morning of February 13, 2017, I got up and took my shower and prepared for my annual mammogram. After I took my shower, I constantly reminded myself not to put on any deodorant because deodorant is not allowed during the mammogram exam, as it can falsely appear as an area of concern. Therefore, I put my deodorant in my purse so that I could apply it afterwards. I dreaded mammograms because the thought of my breasts being smashed, pulled, and touched by a stranger always put me on edge but it was a required exam due to my age.

A few days later, I received my mammogram report in the mail. "Thank you, Jesus," I said, relieved that my results came back negative, with no abnormalities detected.

With the mammogram out of the way, I turned my focus to a more pressing issue: my heavy menstrual flow. I had suffered from this for a couple of years, but it had worsened over the past six months. It was unbearable, often causing me to call in sick to work. It had reached a point where I couldn't cough or sneeze without feeling a gush. Sometimes, I couldn't wear light colored clothing during my menstrual cycle because of the heavy flow. That time of the month often made me feel irritable and it was uncomfortable to sit for long periods of time. Every time I stood up, I wondered if I bled through my clothing. I often felt embarrassed to walk away because of the fear of a stain showing through the back of my pants.

I spent an exorbitant amount of time in the restroom, verifying I hadn't had an accident.

I finally decided that enough was enough and it was time to call my gynecologist. During the office visit with my gynecologist, I explained my symptoms and asked if this was normal. He listened to my concerns and performed an ultrasound on my abdomen by placing that cold gel on my stomach. I immediately had flashbacks of ultrasounds when I was pregnant with my kids, who are now grown adults. After the ultrasound, he told me he had a solution for my problem. I sat up listening enthusiastically with a gleam of hope across my face waiting to hear the gynecologist's solution to my agonizing issue.

He suggested a form of birth control called an Intrauterine Device (IUD). He began to explain to me that the IUD is a small device that fits inside the uterus. "A form of birth control?" I asked. I was surprised, as my fallopian tube was tied since 2002, after the birth of my baby boy via cesarean. He continued to explain that even though my tube was tied, it would help with my heavy menstrual flow. He assured me that I would never experience another heavy menstrual flow again and mentioned that some women no longer have menstrual cycles after getting an IUD. The idea of relief sounded like music to my ears, so I agreed.

The Procedure

March 6, 2017; the day had arrived to resolve my heavy menstrual flow issue. I was both excited and nervous. Nervous because I did not know what to expect or if this procedure would really work. As I lay waiting for the doctor to start, I imagined my life without the heavy flow, a life free of worrying about if I would have an accident and that horrible gush feeling whenever I sneezed or coughed. Finally, I would have some relief. As the doctor put my feet in the stirrups and began the insertion of the IUD, I gripped the side of the gown tightly due to the discomfort, while a tear rolled down my face.

After the procedure, I drove home feeling hot, dizzy, shivering, and in pain. I didn't say a word to my husband, who, along with our two sons, was preparing to go bowling. When he asked if I wanted to join them. I declined, saying I just needed to lay down because of the cramps. I did not want to tell my husband how I was really feeling since he and our sons had planned an evening of fun; I did not want to be a burden. I was experiencing much more than just cramps; this pain was excruciating. I wondered if I made the right decision, and I also wondered if the IUD was in the right place. I took my pain meds and rocked myself to sleep. Days later, the pain and discomfort subsided.

Fast forward to the summer, we were preparing for our middle son's high school graduation and our family cruise. Life seemed to be going well. My heavy menstrual flow was gone, and I felt like a new woman. I no longer need to worry about the heavy flow.

Looking back now, I realize how much those months of relief meant to me. For years, my menstrual flow had been a constant source of stress and embarrassment. The dread of unexpected gushes had controlled many aspects of my life, from choosing dark-colored clothing to declining social invitations. When the IUD seemed to have resolved this issue, I embraced my newfound freedom with enthusiasm. I could plan outings without the nagging fear of an accident, and I no longer felt like my body was betraying me every month. It was a liberating feeling, one that made me appreciate the simple joys of daily life. I felt confident and empowered, ready to tackle new challenges and enjoy time with my family without the shadow of my menstrual woes hanging over me. Everything was going great until I discovered something unusual.

Lump Discovery

On July 24, 2017, while sitting on the sofa with my husband watching TV, I placed my hand on my breast and felt something unusual. I asked my husband to check if he felt it too, and he confirmed it felt like a knot. Concerned, I decided to see my primary care physician the next day.

My primary care physician examined the lump and noted that my mammogram from February had been normal. Nevertheless, he referred me to the breast center for further evaluation. I couldn't believe I was going to the breast center for further testing. I was scared and nervous because this never happened to me before. I tried to think of only good thoughts, believing that this was precautionary. Everything was going to be okay. On July 28, 2017, I received a diagnostic mammogram. After the mammogram, I waited in a small room, the size of a fitting room or smaller. While I put my bra and shirt back on, the technician stopped by and asked me to follow her to a much larger room so that the radiologist could speak with me.

The radiologist came to the larger room and said, "Mrs. Coleman, I reviewed your mammogram, and it looked suspicious." My heart dropped from hearing the word suspicious. He recommended a biopsy to test the lump and discuss the next course of action. While he was talking, my eyes spotted the breast cancer pamphlets on the bookshelf. I remember looking at his mouth as if I could read his lips while he was talking, though it seemed as though the room was silent. All I saw was his mouth moving; the large room appeared to be closing in on me and now the room seemed like it was the size of that changing room.

I informed my family about my biopsy procedure. Everyone sounded encouraging and reassured me that everything was going to be alright. I was scared but I tried not to show the emotions and stress on my face. I told myself to take one day at a time as I waited for the date to have the biopsy done.

Coping with the News

On August 4, 2017, I returned to the breast center for my biopsy. Nervous, I reminded myself that God did

not give me the spirit of fear. As the needle entered my breast to collect a tissue sample, I was ready for it to be over. I kept repeating to myself that God did not give me the spirit of fear, but I noticed how fear was slowly trying to creep into my thoughts. After the biopsy was over, the doctor told me I would receive a phone call in a few days with the results. I prayed fervently for normal results.

On August 8, 2017, while at work, I received the call. The voice on the other end was soft-spoken and pleasant. She informed me that my biopsy results were positive for cancer. Shocked and unable to comprehend, I asked her to repeat it. She provided me with the names of an oncologist and a breast surgeon, but everything she said was a blur. After the call, I ran to the ladies' room and broke down in disbelief; I could not believe the news that I just received. After I exited the ladies' room, I walked into my supervisor's office and closed the door behind me. I sat staring at my supervisor, unable to get any words to come out of my mouth. She asked me if everything was okay. When I opened my mouth to tell her, the tears and uncontrollable crying started. I told her about my results, and she consoled me. She immediately grabbed my hands and started praying. She also told me to go home and take the rest of the day or whatever time I needed off from work. Before I left work, I remember calling my husband and breaking the news to him first, followed by my mom and kids.

When I told my family, they had questions and asked me how I was feeling. I tried my best not to cry or shed a tear around them because I did not want them to worry. I could tell they were trying to maintain their composure around me as well, but I knew it was hard for them to accept the news. In my alone time, I questioned God, asking why this was happening to me. I just could not believe that this was my reality. Whenever I looked at my breast in the mirror, I looked at it in disbelief that cancer resided there.

Deuteronomy 31:6 (NIV), "Be strong and courageous. Do not be afraid or terrified because of them, for the Lord your God goes with you; he will never leave you nor forsake you." provided some comfort during this confusing and distressing time. The following weeks were filled with medical appointments and prayers. Each doctor's visit brought new information. I often felt overwhelmed by the medical jargon and the fast pace at which everything was happening. One moment, I was trying to understand my diagnosis; the next, I was hearing about my treatment plan options. My family and I had countless discussions, weighing the pros and cons of different options. Throughout this process, my husband was my rock. He attended every appointment he could, took meticulous notes, and asked questions I hadn't thought of. His support was unwavering, even as he managed his own fears and anxieties about my health.

The Reveal

A few days after the diagnosis, my husband, youngest son, and my mom (a retired Registered Nurse living in Georgia) joined me for an appointment with the surgeon. The surgeon reassured me that I would be okay and explained that my cancer was stage zero, a non-invasive type called Ductal Carcinoma In Situ (DCIS). My mom rejoiced over the phone, knowing that a stage zero diagnosis was not severe. The surgeon informed me that I would need five weeks of radiation therapy but no chemotherapy. Although relieved, I still wondered how this cancer had developed so quickly.

One restless night, I sought answers from God. I questioned if something I had ingested or inhaled could have caused the cancer. Then, God revealed that it was the birth control. Bewildered, I researched online and found numerous accounts linking the IUD (Mirena) to breast cancer. Many women who had used Mirena to control heavy menstrual flow had developed breast cancer. I shared this revelation with my family and immediately scheduled an appointment to have the IUD removed.

This revelation was a turning point for me. The idea that a medical device meant to improve my quality of life could have contributed to my cancer was both terrifying and infuriating. I felt a mix of betrayal and helplessness. How could something prescribed by my doctor have such dire consequences? I spent countless hours reading stories from other women who had similar experiences (Mirena IUD/ Breast Cancer, 2010). These accounts provided some comfort, knowing I wasn't alone, but they also fueled my determination to have the IUD removed as quickly as possible.

I Survived

Four days after my breast surgery, I had the Mirena IUD removed. The procedure was quick but uncomfortable. My breast surgery was successful, and I completed six weeks of radiation therapy. Additionally, lymph nodes removed from under my armpit tested negative for cancer. Despite the radiation therapy causing discoloration and augmentation of my breast, as well as a raw nipple, I felt relieved.

The surgery itself was a complex and emotionally charged experience. On the morning of the surgery, I was filled with a mix of apprehension and hope. As I was prepped for the operation, the surgical team explained each step to me, ensuring I understood the process. This helped to ease some of my anxiety. They started by administering anesthesia, and soon I was in a deep, dreamless sleep.

When I woke up in the recovery room, I felt groggy and disoriented. The first sensation I noticed was a dull, throbbing pain in my chest where the surgery had taken place. Nurses were attentive, monitoring my vitals and administering pain relief as needed. They encouraged me to take deep breaths and move my arms gently to prevent stiffness. Despite the discomfort, I was relieved that the tumor had been removed and that the surgery was deemed a success.

As the anesthesia wore off, I began to fully realize the impact of the surgery. My chest was bandaged, after having the tumor or mass removed along with some

surrounding breast tissue. The sight of the bandage was unsettling, but the nurses reassured me that it was a normal part of the healing process. The procedure was performed as an outpatient visit or day surgery. The next morning, the nurse called to check on my progress. She was pleased with how the surgery had gone and explained the next steps in my recovery.

Over the next few days, I focused on managing pain and regaining my strength. The first week was the hardest, with frequent discomfort and limited mobility. Simple tasks like getting out of bed or taking a shower required assistance. My husband and mom were incredibly supportive, helping me with daily activities and ensuring I took my medications on time. Their presence provided comfort and strength during these challenging moments.

As the weeks passed, I gradually began to feel better. The bandage was removed, which was a significant milestone in my recovery. My at-home physical therapy sessions helped restore mobility and strength in my arm and shoulder. Although my breast looked different, I embraced these changes as part of my journey toward healing.

However, my original issue of heavy menstrual flow persisted. God led me to find another gynecologist, who discovered three fibroids during a full exam. She offered two options: remove the fibroids or undergo a total hysterectomy. Given my hormone-receptive breast cancer, I opted for the hysterectomy.

The decision to undergo a hysterectomy was not made lightly. It was a major surgery with its own set of risks and recovery challenges. However, the prospect of finally addressing my heavy menstrual flow and eliminating the risk of hormone-related cancer recurrence made it the best choice for me. My new gynecologist was understanding and supportive, explaining every detail of the procedure and what to expect during recovery. Her compassionate care made a significant difference, which helped me face the surgery with confidence.

Reflection

I often wonder why my previous gynecologist didn't discover the fibroids and why he recommended Mirena to stop my flow. Despite these questions, I realize that my journey has given me a powerful story to share. I spoke at a church breast cancer awareness program, encouraging women to pay attention to any abnormalities in their bodies, especially their breasts. My self-breast exam led to the early discovery of my cancer, allowing for successful treatment.

By sharing my experience, I hope to bring awareness and inspire women to advocate for their health. If something feels off, it is crucial to follow up with a healthcare provider immediately. My journey, though challenging, has given me a renewed purpose to educate and support others facing similar battles.

The aftermath of my experiences has taught me invaluable lessons about resilience, self-advocacy, and the

importance of listening to one's body. I've learned that it's essential to question and seek second opinions when something doesn't feel right. My faith played a crucial role in guiding me through this tumultuous period, providing strength and clarity when I needed it most. As I continue to heal and grow, I remain committed to raising awareness about breast cancer and the potential risks associated with certain medical treatments. My story is a testament to the power of early detection, the importance of informed medical decisions, and the strength found in faith and family.

References

Hurskainen, R. S. (2016). Levonorgestrel- releasing intrauterine system and the risk breast cancer: A nationwide cohort study. Acta Oncologica, 55(2), 188-192. doi:10.3109/0284186X.2015.106238

Mirena IUD/ Breast Cancer. (2010, March). Retrieved from The Breast Cancer Community Forum: breastcancer.org

About the Author

Dr. C. Renee Coleman, a distinguished figure in her community, was born and raised in the charming city of Savannah, GA. From an early age, Renee exhibited a profound passion for helping others, a trait that was beautifully illustrated through her dedication to assisting her grandfather with his medications. His affectionate nickname for her, "Nurse Brown," seemed to foreshadow a future in nursing - a profession her mother, Judy, excelled in. However, Renee's journey would ultimately lead her down a different but equally impactful path.

Throughout her life, this innate drive to assist others remained a cornerstone of her identity. Dr. Coleman's career is a testament to her versatile capabilities and strong commitment to service. She has embraced a variety of roles, each allowing her to touch lives in meaningful ways. As a professional mentor, she has guided collegiate students, providing them with the wisdom and support needed to navigate their academic and professional journeys. Her role as an adjunct instructor further showcased her ability to educate and inspire.

Dr. Coleman's expertise is not confined to the academic sphere. She has also served as a financial aid advisor, helping students manage their educational expenses, and as a finance director, where she demonstrated exceptional leadership and financial acumen. In addition to these roles, she channels her passion for exploration and adventure through her independent travel business. As a travel advisor, she specializes in crafting unforgettable vacations for families, enabling them to create cherished memories.

Away from her professional endeavors, Dr. Coleman cherishes time spent with her family, believing deeply in the importance of creating lasting memories. Her move to Arkansas in 2006 marked a significant chapter in her life. It was here that she decided to pursue higher education with renewed vigor. Over the span of seven years, she achieved both her undergraduate and graduate degrees, a feat that underscores her dedication and resilience.

Determined to be the first in her immediate family to earn a doctoral degree, Dr. Coleman's journey was marked by "blood, sweat, and tears." Her relentless pursuit of this goal culminated in a momentous achievement, inspiring those around her and setting a powerful example for future generations.

A life-changing event served as a catalyst for Dr. Coleman to share her story with the world. Through her narrative, she aims to raise awareness and provide encouragement to women everywhere. Her experiences have shaped her into a beacon of strength and perseverance, and she is committed to empowering others by sharing her journey.

Dr. Coleman's favorite motto, "She Believed She Could; So, She Did," perfectly encapsulates her life philosophy. It is a testament to her belief in the power of determination and self-belief.

This motto not only guides her own actions but also serves as an inspiration to those fortunate enough to hear her story.

Today, Dr. C. Renee Coleman resides in Arkansas with her supportive husband, Ron. Together, they continue to build a life filled with love, achievement, and adventure. Her story is a vivid illustration of how passion, perseverance, and a commitment to helping others can lead to a fulfilling and impactful life.

Dr. Coleman has five adult children: Destani, Ron Jr., Shay, Javon, and Kam. She currently has one grandchild, S'Ayon.

For further insights into her journey and to connect with Dr. Coleman, you can reach her at chivondacoleman@yahoo.com or follow her on Facebook under the name DrRenée Coleman.

Quote and Scripture

F-E-A-R has two meanings, **F**orget **E**verything **A**nd **R**un or **F**ace **E**verything **A**nd **R**ise. The choice is yours.-Zig Ziglar

Romans 12:12-"Be joyful in hope, patient in affliction, faithful in prayer."

Chapter 9: The Light Dimmed
By: Crissie Ann Leonard

When you stare into the mirror who is looking back at you? As you struggle to recognize yourself, the mirrored person screams "FRAUD!" Don't think this could happen to you? I didn't either!

As I stared into the mirror hearing those words, tears rolled down my cheeks. They felt hot enough to burn my skin. My watery eyes struggled to focus, and my heart sped up. My breathing became labored as I felt the weight settle on my shoulders, in my heart and in my spirit. I wanted to yell back at her that she was lying but the words stuck in my throat.

I sighed as I realized she was telling the truth. I wasn't a fraud in the sense that I committed a crime or cheated anyone out of anything. The only loss was to my destiny, or so I thought. In reality, I began to buckle from the pressure of my life verse, Matthew 5:14 (NIV), "You are the light of the world. A town built on a hill cannot be hidden."

How do you protect and project your light when you are falling into the darkness from your trauma? I was so deep that I didn't realize how my unaddressed trauma had bound me to a place I didn't know how to escape. And how my new trauma built another layer on my previous ones. A mega-watt smile can distract people from the sadness lingering in my eyes. This was the "game" that I learned to master. My destiny and purpose were the pawns in the game, and I wasn't sure either could survive.

To show you how serious the game was that I was playing, think of Russian Roulette. This is a game of chance played with a gun, bullets, and you. The premise is to load one bullet in the chamber, spin the cylinder, put the muzzle at your temple and pull the trigger. I envisioned that instead of bullets, my rounds would be each trauma I endured and survived. As I pulled the trigger (figuratively), the muzzle fired the trauma "round." Which trauma would be the one to finally remove me from the game? Would it be abandonment, abuse, sexual assault, betrayal, or mourning? Was my faith strong enough to endure this game of chance?

I was saved later in my life and without the full understanding of what that actually meant. I naively believed that my life would be easier and better after giving my life to Christ. A part of me fantasized that only happy times would be ahead. I would have a defined destiny and a purpose that helped people and brought meaning to my life. I needed something greater in my life than the lies of being unloved and unworthy spoken over me. I buried my trauma deep in my soul and chained it there, hoping it never was released back into my life. At the time, I felt that was the only way to cope and live a meaningful life. But buried things tend to rise back up again and mine were no different.

What trauma could be so severe that it could break the chains? Mine was sexual assault. As someone who struggled with self-image and self-esteem issues, the assault was horrendous mentally and physically.

It was a beautiful day in Ohio for a picnic and party. I joined my neighbors for a day of fun times, talks, and bonding moments. Since it was daytime, I didn't lock my door. I planned to be home before dark. I was enjoying myself and lost track of time. The party started to wind down as nighttime approached. It was then that I remembered my house was unlocked. This realization made me uneasy, so I excused myself to go lock the door. I clearly was not thinking straight because I left my phone at my friend's condo. I only took my keys since our condos were close to each other. The party was moving inside so I hurried down the walkway to my place. My head was up, but I wasn't paying attention to my surroundings. I reached my condo and turned to face the door. As I turned, the hair on the back of my neck raised. I paid no attention to that warning as I was focused on locking the door and going back to the other condo. It proved to be MISTAKE!

The next instant I felt hot breath on my neck and hands grabbing me. Before I could process what was happening, I found myself pinned against the wall. My body froze. My voice refused to work except in my mind where I was screaming. His breath fanned my face as his hands began their exploration of my body. He forced his knee between my legs to spread them apart. I was frozen there like a mannequin lifelessly looking out a window.

I spent years surrounded by law enforcement officers, so I knew the moves to defend myself. But in those moments my mind couldn't recall a single one! His exploration turned into fondling and his breath scorched my skin. My voice was still on vacation and refused to work. All I could muster was asking God (in my mind) why this was happening to me again. This phrase was a mantra that kept repeating in my mind. I was "young" in my Christian faith and wasn't sure if God could even hear me. Tears poured from my eyes as he reached for my pants. Even at this point my voice and body refused to do anything to defend myself.

Hearing my cats scratching at the door to get out permeated my mind. Yet, my only thought was that if this moved indoors one of us wasn't coming out. I wasn't sure which one that would be though! I don't recall if he spoke any words during the assault. I know that I didn't, and it took me many years to forgive myself for not screaming for help.

My mental mantra now became please God don't let this happen to me. Why is this happening to me? Telling you that he stopped because I came to my senses and fought back would make me seem strong and it would be a LIE. Instead, a car came into our parking lot and their lights shined on us. He immediately stopped his assault and fled on foot. I still stood frozen to that spot! Some time elapsed and my body and mind awoke from their tranced states.

Now you are thinking surely this is the part where you started screaming. The answer is no. I turned back to the door and opened it to show the cats that I was okay. Then I pet each on their head and closed and locked the door. Turning towards the other condo I made my way down the walkway. I could hear talking and laughter inside, so I tried my best to appear composed and was thinking of an excuse for taking so long to come back. I was sure it could work, but I misjudged how observant my friend was.

I opened the door, came in, and set my keys on his table. Turning the corner into the living room, I saw my friend staring at the doorway where I was. I spoke no words and stood in the doorway for a few moments. He kept staring at me and asked what happened. I just stood there fighting back the tears and unable to speak. His gaze bore into my eyes like he was peering into my soul and mind searching for the answers. I bowed my head as the tears leaked out from my eyes. I didn't want him to see them or see me so vulnerable.

He approached me and stood in front of me. He gently lifted my chin and said, "Tell me what happened." My voice decided to go on vacation again and I remained silent. He said, "open your eyes and tell me what happened." I opened my eyes and met his gaze. It seemed an eternity passed. In reality, a few seconds later he said, "Tell me now!"

There was no way I was going to escape telling him about the assault. So, I swallowed and recounted the events. With each word I could see how angry he was getting. When I finished, he told me to stay there as he stormed out. He locked the door, and I knew he did that not only to keep me safe but to also make sure I didn't try to stop him. He searched the area but to no avail. I asked him if he saw anyone. He said yes; there was a man walking by the tree. I kept silent because I knew if it was that man, my friend would make sure this was his last day on Earth.

We sat on the couch, and he told me it was okay to cry. I asked him not to tell anyone about this event. He wanted me to call the police. I refused. I didn't trust the police due to events from my first marriage. I knew he was upset and frustrated with my decision. We sat there for hours in silence. Finally, I told him I was going home. He escorted me home and checked each room to make sure no one was waiting for me. Once assured that no one was there, he went outside and waited to leave until I locked the door.

I fed my cats and did the dishes. Then I went upstairs to my bedroom. I slumped to the floor and the full impact of what happened hit me. I opened my mouth to silently scream and whimper. Tears poured from my eyes, and I struggled to not hyperventilate. Somehow, I regained control and took a shower. It was a long shower, as I kept trying to scrub the "filth" off my skin. I wanted to burn every inch of my skin off. I could still feel his breath on me and saw the bruising from his assault. When the water ran cold, I got out and dressed in my pajamas. I collapsed on the bed, curled up into a fetal position and cried myself to sleep!

I awoke to my alarm going off for my church reminder. My first thought was that I needed to call my sister and tell her I wasn't going today. I dialed her number and when she picked up, I broke down. I told her I couldn't go to church today. She asked why I was crying. It took a few minutes before I told her I was sexually assaulted the night before outside my condo. I heard the phone drop and her screaming for her husband. He got on the phone and asked what was going on because she was crying and wouldn't say what happened. I told him what I told her, and he said stay there and lock the doors, I am on my way!

He made it to me in record time. He texted me that he was at my door. I went downstairs and let him in. I knew I looked like death warmed over. He looked at me and asked why I didn't call the cops last night. Then he said, "Never mind, I know why, but we are calling them now. Call them now." I dialed the number as I watched him go back outside. I knew he was outside looking for "clues." He came back upset and we waited for the police. The officer arrived and took a report. It was not a pleasant experience! My brother-in-law called my sister, and they talked for a while. I told them I wanted to stay home and sleep. They reluctantly agreed. I did my best to assure them that I was going to be okay. In no way was I going to tell them that every time I closed my eyes, I relived that attack. I wasn't even sure if or when I would ever be okay, but I kept that to myself.

The police contacted me a week later saying they didn't find the perpetrator. They knew he approached me from behind a parked van. He wasn't from our area but was at a party two complexes away. They advised that this case was stagnant and wouldn't be explored any further.

Later that month, my sister called to tell me the moving arrangements were made. I was confused because I didn't plan on moving but she had other ideas. She contacted my landlord and told him it was a safety concern for me to stay there and submitted my intention to leave. We packed my condo and a week later they arrived with the moving truck. This part of my life had ended. They felt a change of scenery would do me good. However, I knew this move was more for my safety and their peace of mind. They wanted me close in case I spiraled out of control. So, off to their house I went with my two cats.

Over the next few months, I learned how to mask my pain and torment. On the outside I appeared to be "healing" well. The bruises started to fade, and I started to participate in life again. What they didn't know was that on the inside, I was a mess and broken. My mind felt fractured, as if part of it kept reliving the event and another part tried to protect me from the memories. I knew I needed to seek professional help, so I contacted a Christian counselor in a nearby town.

I felt comfortable with her as soon as I walked into her office. I can't say exactly why other than my spirit felt relief. She worked with me for months as she slowly peeled back the layers of the trauma. During one session, she told me to go to a retreat that was down the street. It was for sexual assault and rape survivors. I knew that this was not a request but a veiled demand. I smiled and agreed to go.

The moment I walked into the event I felt at home. Here before me where women who understood the tormented journey I was on. We were all kindred spirits. I believe that retreat saved me by putting me on a different course in my life. Taking the first step into that room set me on a healing journey.

I kept attending the group meetings after the retreat. One of my dearest friends came from that group. I even had an opportunity to speak at a Take Back the Night SARN event at a local college. The first stage of my healing had begun. Learning to work through the emotional and mental pain was a huge step!

I was still uncomfortable in social settings. The idea of being in close contact with anyone made me edgy. Yet, I knew I had to find a way to overcome this obstacle. I was always one to respond to challenges, so I knew that I needed to reintegrate back into society. I was determined that the fear and horrific memories would not control me for the rest of my life.

I learned what my trauma triggers were and how to respond to them. I enrolled in a R.A.D. (Rape Aggression Defense) classes. They taught you self-defense moves and spoke to you on how to defend yourself during an attack or kidnapping attempt. We were in combat gear and had simulations. To "graduate" you had to go through scenario training. Being an overachiever at that time, I wanted to go first. However, I ended up helping the other women gear up and gave them pep talks. I figured that the officer would be worn out when the last student came in. That student was me and was I ever wrong in that thought process!

This officer was domineering to look at. He was all muscle and outweighed me by at least 50 pounds! We had to do three scenarios, each one harder than the previous. The first one was yelling for help. Coincidentally my voice decided to take part in that one! The second one was maneuvering, which I passed. The third one I dreaded-it was his choice. I was closer to the leader of R.A.D. and she knew story. Somehow, I felt with every fiber of my being that I was going to be in an assault from behind scenario. This time I trusted my instincts and they proved to be correct.

In this scenario I had my back to him since I was enacting an ATM withdrawal. My back was turned to him. I was hyperaware and yet trying not to hyperventilate. He grabbed me from behind and took me down to the mat. He maneuvered to be on top and our gear came off. That meant we had to start over. I told myself I could do this. It was only a "friendly" attack so how bad could it get? Don't ever ask yourself a question that you don't want the answer to!

I moved back into the ATM position. I wasn't prepared for his approach as I was still giving myself a pep talk. This time he took me by surprise when his arm circled around my waist. I froze! As I fought against the numbness spreading through my body from fear, I found myself turned around and going airborne before being thrown on the mat. This time I was on top and couldn't move. Fear gripped me as the memories assaulted me. He knew what was happening with me and made a move that further terrified me. I felt his breath near my neck as he uttered the words, "you are mine" in my ear!

I don't know if it was the words or how he said them, but my mind cleared, and I heard my fellow participants yelling for me and cheering me on. A switch flipped on in my mind and body. I was a rabid dog in a street fight. Adrenaline coursed through my veins, and I fought back like a madwoman. I landed blow after blow on him, and he kept fighting back. We were still on the ground, and I knew to graduate I had to flip him over me when we stood up. Every move we rehearsed flowed into my mind. I maneuvered out of his grip and made it to my feet. He stalked me like a predator surrounding its prey. He charged me and I knew this was my one chance to make my move. As he approached, I lowered my body into position to grab him and initiate the flip. Now, you could not tell who the predator was and who was the prey!

I heard the women and the instructor screaming, "FLIP HIM!" He got close and I initiated the flip move, got him over my back and onto the mat. On his way down, I threw one head shot that missed his face guard and hit his nose. I escaped his grip and made it to the safe area. The thunderous applause and seeing him on the mat brought a triumphant smile to my lips.

I went over to check on him. He stood up, wiped his nose, and smiled. He told me he felt the change in me when he said the words in my ear. Then he smiled like a proud papa. He told me that I was stronger than I thought and congratulated me for passing. I finally felt I could live a somewhat normal life and knew how to defend myself now.

Next, I decided to find ways to become one with society again. Plus, I had to get a grip on my fear of dark places. It seemed the dark issue would be easier to master. I started parking under lights in parking lots, kept my head up while walking to stay alert, and carried my keys in a manner to use as weapons if needed. I went to the movies to overcome my flight or fright response. Slowly, that trigger minimized. I still don't enter dark places and struggle to sleep in rooms that are completely dark.

Now the biggest obstacle of how to be comfortable in society again... I went to dinner by myself and observed how people acted in public. I watched how they interacted with each other, studied their mannerisms, and listened to the conversations around me. At the beginning, I set in the back and over time, I gradually moved into the more populated areas. I asked my few male friends to accompany me places or spend time with me so I could work on being in close proximity to men. It took a long time, and I eventually found my comfort level in society and in men being around me.

Eventually the images faded from my dreams, the memories became reminders to be cautious when out by myself, and my friendships with the few men in my life deepened. I addressed the trauma and learned how it affected my mind and body. My faith deepened and I realized that a miracle did happen on the day of the attack. The miracle was the car pulling into the parking lot. It stopped the attack and saved my life. I realized that God started filling in the broken pieces of me with His love.

The counselor taught me that I didn't do anything to bring that event onto myself. God showed me He could use the trauma for a greater purpose. That event didn't make me unlovable or unworthy for the purpose He has in my life. It left scars to remind me of the battle I endured. The assault took many things from me and caused me pain, emotionally, mentally, and physically.

Yet, it also made me deepen my faith, become someone new, and becoming a spokesperson on surviving and thriving after sexual assault. An incident that was meant to destroy me instead, over time, made me stronger. The healing was the first step onto the path to my purpose. God used that horrific event and turned it into a powerful testimony!

My light dimmed that day and for a long time after it. At times, it was only a flicker, but it refused to be extinguished. I finally understood that my life verse was never meant to be a pressure-producing burden, but a testament to my story of survival. Sometimes my light shines as a bright beacon to others like a lighthouse shines into the dark seas at night. Other times, it is a flicker like a candle. Just enough to be seen. Whether it is bright or a flicker, my light continues shine for God's Kingdom. My story could have ended in tragedy, but instead it breathes life into a hope that endures!

About the Author

Crissie Ann Leonard is an author who has loved literature since she could read. Building on that love and personal experiences, her writing focuses on life, faith, growth, and healing.

She has been a lifelong writer and first began with short stories and poetry, only to be sidetracked by life—joy and sorrow, love, and loss. When God's purpose rose to meet her pain, her journey began.

Author, Letters to My Father

Author, Color My Feelings Scripture Coloring Book

Author, Names of God Devotional Coloring Book

Author, Your Story Matters Writing Journal

Author, It the Write Time Writing Prompt Guide

Founder-It's the Write Time Author Group

Featured in Triumphant Magazine

Reader's Favorite Book Award Finalist

Ohioana Book Festival Author

Writing Coach/Mentor

SARN Take Back the Night Speaker

HAMS Career Day Speaker

Film Festival Winner-YMP Creations Jewelry Commercial

Animal Lover

Christ Follower

Collaborator

<u>Connect with me:</u>

Facebook: Crissie Ann Leonard

Instagram: @crissieauthor

TikTok:@humbleheartbeat

YouTube: @thehumbleheartbeat

Email:info@crissieleonard.com

Quote and Scripture

Light and shadow are opposite sides of the same coin. We can illuminate our paths or darken our way. It is a matter of choice.-Maya Angelou

Romans 12:12-"Be joyful in hope, patient in affliction, faithful in prayer."

My Sister's and Brother's Keepers

Thank you for reading this book. Hearing survival stories gives us hope. Seeing how God moves in people's live strengthens our faith.

For those reasons we created My Sister's and Brother's Keeper. We wanted to create a platform that addresses the need to:

> Break poverty generational curses

> Bring unity to the Body of Christ

> Bring Ministry and the Marketplace Together

Both Calvin and I hope to continue this journey for years to come. Our desire is to inspire others to take a step to break the chains that bind them and change their lives.

We hope you will join us at a future event and become part of this movement!

With love,

Tiffany McIntosh

Calvin McIntosh

Psalm 91(NIV):

"Whoever dwells in the shelter of the Most High will rest in the shadow of the Almighty. I will say of the Lord, "He is my refuge and my fortress, my God, in whom I trust. Surely he will save you from the fowler's snare and from the deadly pestilence. He will cover you with his feathers, and under his wings you will find refuge; his faithfulness will be your shield and rampart. You will not fear the terror of night, nor the arrow that flies by day, nor the pestilence that stalks in the darkness, nor the plague that destroys at midday. A thousand may fall at your side, ten thousand at your right hand, but it will not come near you. You will only observe with your eyes and see the punishment of the wicked. If you say, "The Lord is my refuge," and you make the Most High your dwelling, no harm will overtake you, no disaster will come near your tent. For he will command his angels concerning you to guard you in all your ways; they will lift you up in their hands, so that you will not strike your foot against a stone. You will tread on the lion and the cobra; you will trample the great lion and serpent. "Because he loves me," says the Lord, "I will rescue him; I will protect him, for he acknowledges my name. He will call on me, and I will answer him; I will be with him in trouble, I will deliver him and honor him. With long life I will satisfy him and show him my salvation."

www.ingramcontent.com/pod-product-compliance
Lightning Source LLC
Chambersburg PA
CBHW060406030726
47497CB00003B/863